Devil's Advocates

DEVIL'S ADVOCATES is a series of books devoted to exploring the classics of horror cinema. Contributors to the series come from the fields of teaching, academia, journalism and fiction, but all have one thing in common: a passion for the horror film and a desire to share it with the widest possible audience.

'The admirable Devil's Advocates series is not only essential – and fun – reading for the serious horror fan but should be set texts on any genre course.'
Dr Ian Hunter, Reader in Film Studies, De Montfort University, Leicester

'Auteur Publishing's new Devil's Advocates critiques on individual titles... offer bracingly fresh perspectives from passionate writers. The series will perfectly complement the BFI archive volumes.' **Christopher Fowler,** *Independent on Sunday*

'Devil's Advocates has proven itself more than capable of producing impassioned, intelligent analyses of genre cinema... quickly becoming the go-to guys for intelligent, easily digestible film criticism.' *HorrorTalk.com*

'Auteur Publishing continue the good work of giving serious critical attention to significant horror films.' *Black Static*

ALSO AVAILABLE IN THIS SERIES

A Girl Walks Home Alone at Night Farshid Kazemi

Black Sunday Martyn Conterio

The Blair Witch Project Peter Turner

Blood and Black Lace Roberto Curti

The Blood on Satan's Claw David Evans-Powell

Candyman Jon Towlson

The Cabin in the Woods Susanne Kord

Cannibal Holocaust Calum Waddell

Cape Fear Rob Daniel

Carrie Neil Mitchell

The Company of Wolves James Gracey

The Conjuring Kevin J. Wetmore Jr.

Creepshow Simon Brown

Cruising Eugenio Ercolani & Marcus Stiglegger

The Curse of Frankenstein Marcus K. Harmes

Daughters of Darkness Kat Ellinger

Dawn of the Dead Jon Towlson

Dead of Night Jez Conolly & David Bates

The Descent James Marriot

The Devils Darren Arnold

Don't Look Now Jessica Gildersleeve

The Evil Dead Lloyd Haynes

The Fly Emma Westwood

Frenzy Ian Cooper

Halloween Murray Leeder

House of Usher Evert Jan van Leeuwen

In the Mouth of Madness Michael Blyth

IT: Chapters 1 & 2 Alissa Burger

It Follows Joshua Grimm

Ju-on The Grudge Marisa Hayes

Let the Right One In Anne Billson

M Samm Deighan

Macbeth Rebekah Owens

The Mummy Doris V. Sutherland

Nosferatu Cristina Massaccesi

The Omen Adrian Schober

Peeping Tom Kiri Bloom Walden

Pet Sematary Shellie McMurdo

Possession Alison Taylor

Re-Animator Eddie Falvey

Repulsion Jeremy Carr

Saw Benjamin Poole

Scream Steven West

The Shining Laura Mee

Shivers Luke Aspell

The Silence of the Lambs Barry Forshaw

Snuff Mark McKenna

Suspiria Alexandra Heller-Nicholas

The Texas Chain Saw Massacre James Rose

The Thing Jez Conolly

Trouble Every Day Kate Robertson

Twin Peaks: Fire Walk With Me Lindsay Hallam

Witchfinder General Ian Cooper

FORTHCOMING

The Craft Miranda Corcoran

I Walked with a Zombie Clive Dawson

The Wicker Man Steve A. Wiggins

Devil's Advocates

Poltergeist

Rob McLaughlin

ACKNOWLEDGEMENTS

The first film to give me nightmares.

I would like to thank my parents for letting me stay up and watch *Poltergeist* when it was on television. I would also like to apologise to them for problems that this decision made for them in tending to my nightmares afterwards.

First published in 2023 by
Auteur, an imprint of
Liverpool University Press,
4 Cambridge Street,
Liverpool
L69 7ZU

Series design: Nikki Hamlett at Cassels Design
Set by Cassels Design, Luton UK
Printed and bound by CPI Group (UK) Ltd, Croydon CR0 4YY

All rights reserved. No part of this publication may be reproduced in any material form (including photocopying or storing in any medium by electronic means and whether or not transiently or incidentally to some other use of this publication) without the permission of the copyright owner.

British Library Cataloguing-in-Publication Data
A catalogue record for this book is available from the British Library

ISBN hardback: 9781800856974
ISBN paperback: 9781800856981
eISBN: 9781800857452

CONTENTS

Figures vi

Preface 1

Chapter 1: They're here 5

Chapter 2: The evolution of suburban horror 19

Chapter 3: Tricksters and fairy tales 33

Chapter 4: The American Dream/The American Nightmare—The politics

    of *Poltergeist* 57

Chapter 5: Television and trauma 71

Chapter 6: Matriarchy and monsters—The importance of family and the feminine 85

Chapter 7: Cultural resonance and conclusions 99

Bibliography 111

FIGURES

Figure 1.1. The Freelings 7

Figure 1.2. Spielberg suburbia 15

Figure 2.1. Housing estate 25

Figure 2.2. Estate overview 31

Figure 3.1. Ask Dad 39

Figure 3.2. The clown 44

Figure 3.3. Storm 48

Figure 3.4. Sinister tree 50

Figure 3.5. The Beast 55

Figure 4.1. The Freelings's lifestyle 61

Figure 4.2. Blue-collar intrusion 68

Figure 5.1. 'The TV people' 74

Figure 5.2. Horror in the mirror 81

Figure 6.1. Diane Freeling, the heroine 87

Figure 6.2. Female hierarchy 92

Figure 6.3. Birth and rebirth 95

Figure 7.1. Final scene 106

Figure 7.2. The Simpsons' parody 109

Preface

The Academy Award-winning *Poltergeist* (1982), created by Steven Spielberg and directed by Tobe Hooper, is a film that can be framed as a cinematic anomaly—a high-budget, high-profile Hollywood summer blockbuster and a film that can also be categorised as a legitimate horror movie.

Upon its release in 1982 *Poltergeist* was promoted in a somewhat disingenuous fashion—presented very much as a film that would appeal towards the viewing habits of a family audience. This misnomer (as *Poltergeist* is very much not a family-friendly movie) can be evidenced by the film's initial pre-release and marketing preamble, which played significantly on Steven Spielberg's high-profile involvement in the film's production. This duplicity in the promotion of the film to garner audiences' interest does in some way provide a reflection to the actual narrative of the film itself in which the supernatural protagonists use guile and trickery to achieve their goals. While the film studio is, of course, not a malevolent child-abducting supernatural entity, *Poltergeist* as a text differs significantly from its kindred films, possessing neither the feel-good uplifting positivity of *Close Encounters of the Third Kind* (1977) nor *E.T. the Extra-Terrestrial* (*E.T.*) (1982) but was, in many ways, promoted as such. Described by Newman (1988) as the 'horror equivalent of the exuberant, harmless, greatest show on earth genre blockbusters', on reflection the film is not the jovial experience that some critics have made it out to be, as Muir's (2002) take certainly highlights, contradicting this opinion by describing the film as filled with extremities and containing 'a terrifying concoction of horror thrills and chills'.

It is with these diametrically opposing standpoints that the film's sense of duality, dichotomy, and contradiction can be framed. It is a film that is both spine-tingling yet 'safe'—a 'gateway' text into the realm of horror but one that shows a willingness to push boundaries in implied and explicit horror. *Poltergeist* is a film framed by paradoxes; from its inception, production, and narrative there is a continual sense of contradiction. Audiences, reviewers, and critics alike have found it hard to define and categorise the film—as it is an outright horror, family adventure film, blockbuster, and grindhouse text all at the same time.

It could be argued that the film's difficultly to be categorised and defined comes from the text's unique creative synergy behind the camera. The production of *Poltergeist* while

DEVIL'S ADVOCATES

overseen by Steven Spielberg was not directed by him—with Tobe Hooper chosen to direct the feature. Both creatives had in their own way already provided significant cultural resonance with their prior works even before production of *Poltergeist* had begun. Spielberg, by then the more famous of the duo, had instilled an abject fear of open water onto an entire generation of filmgoers by providing legitimate blockbuster terror via the unseen horrors lurking just below the waterline via *Jaws* (1975). In comparison Hooper's own contribution to the tapestry of cinematic culture came via the arid deserts of southern America via *The Texas Chain Saw Massacre* (1974), a film that Bloom (2004) has described as 'cultural shorthand for perversity, moral decline, and especially the corruption of children'.

This framing of *Poltergeist* as an inconsistent text and one that pushes the boundaries of cinematic acceptability can also be seen within the film's troubled journey through the global cinema rating and film classification systems. The film is notorious for being the text that redefined censorship, as well as bringing into question the decision-making processes of the board of the Motion Picture Association of America (MPAA). Initially released in America as an R-rated film (under 18s must be accompanied by an adult), Spielberg lobbied the board for the film's harsh (and in some way understandable) rating. Eventually this initial classification was overturned from its initial rating to bring the film down to a questionable (but much more financially lucrative) PG certification. This decision, spearheaded by MPAA member Jack Valenti, holds that *Poltergeist* as a film is 'all threat and fantasy, not reality' (Brook, 2001).

In the UK the British Board of Film Classification (BBFC) initially certificated the film with an X rating (barring anyone under 18) while arguably it could have been certified at the lower AA rating (barring anyone under 14). These decisions made on the release of the film in 1982 were subsequently amended with the introduction of the PG-13 in 1984, a certification that again Spielberg had some influence in framing with the release of his *Indiana Jones and the Temple of Doom* (1984). As such *Poltergeist* now resides at this rating in the United States and is recertificated as a 15 within the United Kingdom.

Poltergeist presented as this paradoxical curious cinematic anomaly, discussed far more within the pages of *Rue Morgue* and *Fangoria* than in copies of *Variety* or *Empire*, is, at its heart, a classic modern take on the traditional haunted house story. It is a film that as

Latham (1994) states delivers both Hooper's corrosive contempt for the bourgeois and Spielberg's suburban fixation, allowing both Spielberg and Hooper to bring something creatively unique to the 1970s/early 1980s modern horror genre. It is a film that mixes both the horrific and the satirical and provides the audience with both justifiable jump scares and a morality tale of the importance of the love for family over material goods.

Chapter 1: They're here

'Metro-Goldwyn-Mayer presents a Steven Spielberg production, a Tobe Hooper film, "Poltergeist," starring Jobeth Williams, Craig T. Nelson and Beatrice Straight'
(Official Press Material)

Described as a 'family' horror movie throughout its production schedule and marketed as such via the film's public relations (PR) and press, the promotional material for *Poltergeist* focused heavily on Spielberg's involvement in the film. Described by Kellner (1983b) as one of the most identifiable effective cinematic chroniclers of affluent middle-class lifestyle, it was inevitable that any promotion of *Poltergeist* by MGM focused on the name and reputation of Spielberg. While Spielberg is credited as the producer of the film, he is also credited for the film's initial story and screenplay. It is the renowned grindhouse auteur Tobe Hooper, whose prior works had been described as an 'expression of the assaultive' (BFI, 2017), who according to the official paperwork of the film is credited as *Poltergeist*'s director.

This relatively simplistic credit association is, however, also a little more complex than the film's posters, interviews, and publicity material may first appear. The development, production, and post-production of the film by this duo of filmmakers, whose styles at first seem to be diametrically opposed to each other, is rather more convoluted and intertwined, adding again to the text's themes of paradoxes, complexities, and contradictions. While the varying debates surrounding who actually directed the film could fill another volume of work, the 'known facts', stated via the official production credits for *Poltergeist* (as noted at the beginning of this chapter), are the baseline for initially exploring this Spielberg/Producer—Hooper/Director dynamic.

This official presentation again is also not without its own controversy. A legal stipulation on contractual obligations decreed that if any marketing or promotional material regarding the film utilised Steven Spielberg's name it had to use Tobe Hooper's name as well—in equal prevalence. Evidence, however, from numerous sources published at the time, including the film's official press-books, provide numerous examples of this not occurring when citing *Poltergeist*'s cinematic credentials; only once in a very small piece is Hooper's name evident with the same credence as Spielberg's.

The end credit roll of *Poltergeist* surprisingly also fails to acknowledge Hooper as the director of the film. The initial ident notes that *Poltergeist* is a 'Steven Spielberg Production' then moves directly to acknowledge that Kathleen Kennedy is the associate producer of the film. The credits continue to roll, proceeding directly to acknowledge the casting and first and second assistant director roles—knowingly and by intended design leaving Hooper's name off this credit roll completely.

With these continual contravening presentations of the film via press, publicity, and marketing as well as the potentially deliberate removal of Hooper as an end credit directorial acknowledgement it is no wonder that people mistakenly still assume (even after four decades) that *Poltergeist* is a Steven Spielberg 'directed' film rather than a Tobe Hooper directed production.

1.1 THE PLOT

The plot and framing of *Poltergeist* provide a narrative purposely set in both location and tone to intentionally portray the concepts of normalcy. The film, while eventually deviating and unfolding into the extraordinary and into a quintessential modern horror movie, purposely tricks the viewer into a false sense of security by its initial portrayal of tranquil suburban surroundings. Crafting this purposefully familiar setting via what can be described as an 'idyllic suburbia' intentionally enhances the aspects of the 'extra'-ordinary seen later in the film. From the seemingly benevolent 'TV-People' to the duplicitous actions of Carol Anne's supernatural abduction to the other unearthly manifestations of aggressive malevolence and anger via the depiction of 'The Beast', the film intentionally lulls its viewer into a false sense of comfort and relatability—meaning that the events that transpire within the text are that much more impactful.

The protagonists of the film, the Freelings, are presented as a typical American 'nuclear family', consisting of the archetypal 2.4 children. Overseeing the family is patriarch Steven, portrayed by Craig T. Nelson. Depicted as a loving father and working family man his job is that of a senior sales executive for a 'Real Estate' company—debatably the main antagonists of the film. In the context of the film plot his well-paid role is one of selling near identical properties on the new vast Californian housing estate on which he and his family also live.

Figure 1.1. The Freelings

The rest of the family, which includes his wife Diane (played by JoBeth Williams), teenage daughter Dana (Dominique Dunne), and two younger children Robbie (Oliver Robbins) and Carol Anne (Heather O'Rouke), share a large house in this affluent neighbourhood of Cuesta Verde, California with a dog EBuzz, a goldfish, and a bird Tweety (deceased during the story).

The film's premise focuses on the Freelings's confrontation with an external supernatural force—namely a 'poltergeist', which initially appears as a relativity benign curiosity transmitted through the television to their youngest daughter Carol Anne. While portrayed initially as benevolent these supernatural forces are in fact malevolent entities that proceed to abduct Carol Anne from her family, trapping her on the 'Other Side'—a realm of the dead ruled by a horrific presence described as 'The Beast'.

With no way rational way of getting their daughter, the family turn to an unorthodox team of parapsychologists to investigate her disappearance, resorting eventually to requesting the aid of the powerful medium Tangina Barrons to oversee a rescue attempt of Carol Anne from the 'Other Side'.

It is in this rescue that we see Diane travel to the 'Other Side' via a portal in Carol Anne's wardrobe to rescue her daughter while the remaining family members are confronted by a monstrous apparition of The Beast. Navigating the 'Other Side' Diane and the family succeed in rescuing Carol Anne and, having participated in such a traumatic event, the family are keen to leave the house as soon as possible. During the final preparations to

DEVIL'S ADVOCATES

finally move out of the house the spirits, angry at losing Carol Anne and her 'light', once again attempt to re-capture her and, as revenge for their loss physically assault Diane and angrily uproot up the dead bodies buried beneath the house.

The finale of the film reveals that the poltergeist's supernatural disturbances and Carol Anne's abduction are due to the real estate company Steven works for, which have been building houses, such as the one the Freelings themselves live in, over a mass graveyard. In this attempt to increase profitability it is revealed that the company habitually cut corners, removing only the headstones from the graves of the graveyard and not exhuming and reburying the bodies below it. It is with this horrific knowledge that Steven angrily confronts his boss Teague, violently admonishing him with the lines, 'You moved the cemetery. But you left the bodies, didn't you! You son-of-a-bitch, you left the bodies and only moved the headstones!' as, in a final act of spite the spirits aggressively rip apart the family home piece by piece, eventually imploding the house entirely into a ball of supernatural energy.

This notion of the corporate pursuit of profit by any means necessary is seen as one of the underlying themes of the text—which can be framed as a social critique of the perils of capitalism and the growth of the lack of responsibility in the pursuit of the 'greed is good' mentality. The corporate greed sub-text presented in the film evidences the political shift towards this mindset in the late 1970s, reinforced by the Ronald Reagan 'free market' economic model that had been driven by the President during this time. This political standpoint encouraged the drive for corporate profitability no matter the moral or social cost—usually without thought or foresight of the consequences that these actions would cause. This drive by a faceless corporate entity to purposely pursue this agenda—driven by shareholders, dividends, and profit—provide the text with the film's real antagonist. It is not the varying spirits or indeed The Beast who—while being terrifying supernatural creations themselves—are the real 'monster' of the film; bringing the wider troubles and trauma to the Freeling family is a much more tangible and down to earth 'monster': a greedy corporation whose pursuit of profit supersedes any or all notion of societal well-being—a fate that a lot of the audience viewing *Poltergeist* for the first time in 1982 were becoming acutely aware of.

From the opening scenes depicting the Freelings's opulent loving environment to the finale of the film that sees them lose everything the film's power and impact is derived from this ensemble cast's wholly convincing portrayal of trauma though loss and their desperate turn to any means necessary to reunite their family and pull together in the face of adversity. No matter how extraordinary the film's concepts are it is these aspects of the portrayal of a realistic loving family that is arguably where the film's success lies. The direction by Hooper and portrayal by the cast in creating the Freelings who confront and overcome forces intent on tearing them apart is one that resonated with the audience who instantly garnered sympathy for their unnatural predicament.

1.2 THE ORIGINS OF THE FILM

Steven Spielberg's breakthrough into the Hollywood mainstream came via Universal Pictures with *Jaws*, a text that significantly impacted on an entire generation of cinematic audiences, catapulting the director into A-List status. Having already proven his directorial acumen with *Duel* (1971) and *The Sugarland Express* (1974), *Jaws* proved not only to be a huge box-office success for Universal but also resonated with its vast social impact. Spielberg now garnered significant influence within the Hollywood studio system and, as such, was able to move forward with the first of his suburban trilogy, *Close Encounters of the Third Kind*, for Columbia.

While Spielberg's trajectory towards Hollywood success has been well documented Tobe Hooper's career took a very much more varied route to gain cinematic success and acclaim. The director's breakthrough film *The Texas Chain Saw Massacre*, while heavily criticised at the time, gained Hooper the reputation as a counter-culture 'grindhouse auteur' with the film now nearly five decades after its release being deemed to be one of the most significant texts in the lexicon of cinematic horror.

Hooper's directorial projects prior to *Poltergeist*, which included *Eaten Alive* (1976) and *The Funhouse* (1981), brought the director neither the critical acclaim of his first feature nor significant box-office returns. While the made-for-television *Salem's Lot* (1979) garnered the director much acclaim on the smaller screen it was only with *Poltergeist* that the director really made his mainstream breakthrough into the Hollywood studio system, allowing him to direct other features such as *Lifeforce* (1985) and the remake of *Invaders from Mars* (1986). It was not only Hooper's ability to invoke fear in his audience in his prior work that gained him the reputation and skill to handle the directorial reins

DEVIL'S ADVOCATES

of *Poltergeist*; it was also his ability in his films to portray a critique of modern America. His prior repertoire of films had challenged the evolving social and political landscape of modern living that Spielberg saw and acknowledged in allowing Hooper to direct his screenplay.

It was essential in the directorial choice of *Poltergeist* that the individual provided an understanding of the themes and sub-text of the perils of consumerism and modern life evident in Spielberg's initial draft of the film. In Hooper, Spielberg saw a kindred spirit that would allow the film to not only be framed as a modern horror film but also to provide the acumen to properly present the text as a morality tale in which these deliberate aspects of social satire are present to highlight the notion for the need to embrace loved ones rather than material goods.

Within the production credits of the film Spielberg is not given *complete* acknowledgement for the writing of the film (he is noted in credit for writing the screenplay only); however, this lack of associated credit aside does not mean that he was not significantly influential in the development of the script for the film, writing three differing script treatments that would eventually become the screenplay for both *E.T.* and *Poltergeist*.

During the late 1970s Spielberg had developed a set of variant screenplays entitled *Night-Time/Night Skies/It's Night Time*, which were initially conceived as concepts that could be developed into an unofficial sequel to *Close Encounters of the Third Kind*. The varying treatments, plots, themes, and details can be seen over iterations to evolve into both the final screenplays for both *E.T.* and *Poltergeist* with the *Night-Time* screenplay focusing on a remote rural farming family terrorised by aliens. The initial theme of aggressive aliens eventually turned into one of benevolent extra-terrestrial presence for *E.T.* and the aspects of a family besieged by malevolent forces were developed into the eventual screenplay of *Poltergeist*.

While both screenplays diverged in tone at an early stage, both still share common themes and traits on their separate journeys to development and eventual production with both screenplays eventually relocating their settings from a remote farmhouse to a new modern Californian suburb. The final treatment for *E.T.*'s screenplay was passed into the hands of Melissa Mathison for a final re-write, eventually becoming the much more family orientated science-fiction blockbuster. The darker, more sinister elements

10

presented in *Night-Time* were taken by Spielberg into the first draft script for *Poltergeist*. The screenplay that would eventually become Poltergeist saw the move away from a family in seclusion and instead pursued a narrative based in suburbia, focusing instead on a haunting rather than alien encounter. Throughout all the iterations of the script the main narrative in which a young family are tormented by an external malevolent force was consistent, however the amendment that changed extra-terrestrial entities to supernatural entities allowed for iconic (and visual effects heavy) set pieces, such as the spirits floating down the stairs and the swimming pool scene, to be developed and storyboarded in significant detail before production. The screenplay continued through various iterations and treatments eventually being green lit into production. The final screenplay writing credits for the film were eventually given to Michael Grais and Mark Victor—based on Steven Spielberg's treatments.

The screenplay of *Poltergeist* is also not a purely unique idea but rather a modern-day take on the haunted house scenario, using the 'traditional quest' tropes described in Joseph Campbell's 'Monomyth' (Kendrick, 2009). The film was also heavily influenced by other writers, especially those who worked in serialised science fiction throughout the 1950s and 1960s. Works that can be seen to be an influence on *Poltergeist* screenplay range from works by acclaimed writers such as Richard Matheson's 'Through Channels' (1951), which sees a family attacked by creatures from the television set and the *Twilight Zone* episode 'Little Girl Lost' (Season 3, 1962) based on a story first published in *Amazing Stories Magazine* (1953), which sees a child disappear without trace in a family's home. His other work on the show, which includes 'The Invaders' (Season 2—1961), 'Mute' (Season 4—1963), and 'Night-Call' (Season 5—1964), also provide examples of the medium of household objects and family homes being used as conduits or weapons by the invasive other-worldly entities.

Other examples of derivative aspects of *Poltergeist*'s screenplay include the notion of voices 'from beyond' picked up via broadcast, which are also present in *The Changeling* (1980) and Diane's traumatic molestation by an invisible antagonist that resembles elements presented in the contemporaneously released *The Entity* (1982). As such, while *Poltergeist* is a modern reinterpretation of a traditional haunted house tale it can also be seen as an amalgam of prior works and ideas, reconstituted via Spielberg's science-fiction and fantasy influences.

In January of 1980 screenwriter Paul Clemens alleged that he submitted a script treatment to Spielberg's production company, Amblin Entertainment, which featured a girl trapped somewhere beneath a house. The child's disappearance provides the revelation that the house the family live in is built on a drained swamp that contains dead bodies, which, during the climax of the script, rise from the grave. The screenplay's themes of lost children and abduction mirror *Poltergeist*'s key plot themes, as too does the finale of the film in which the dead bodies buried beneath the Freelings's house rise up through the floor.

Spielberg, whose work is often framed—rightly or wrongly—as stereotypically American whimsical fantasy (Gordon, 2008), serves up a narrative of a much darker hue in *Poltergeist*. This darkness of context can be found in *Duel* and, of course, *Jaws*, as well as his early televisual offerings, such as *Something Evil* (1972)—a script that in many ways can be read as a prototype for *Poltergeist*, as it too portrays a family living in a haunted house whose child goes missing. What makes *Poltergeist* different as a text from these other Spielbergian works, however, is not the implied notions of horror but the purposeful insertion of more visceral abhorrent scenes on-screen. While there is no denying that the jump-scare of discovering Ben Gardner's severed head or the gruesome death of Quint in *Jaws* are shocking, the transgressive visuals of *Poltergeist*, including bodily mutilation, physical sexual attacks, and images of decomposition, push the aesthetic of *Poltergeist* way beyond the perceived safety of prior Spielberg texts. While these representations of on-screen excess and extremity could be debated to be present due to the directorial decisions made by Hooper, he had no hand in the development of the screenplay of the film with his task being to direct Spielberg's screenplay, which already contained all these aspects of the abhorrent.

1.3 *POLTERGEIST* AS PART OF THE SPIELBERG 'SUBURBAN TRILOGY'

Released as the middle entry of Spielberg's 1980s cycle of texts that juxtapose the idyllic setting of modern middle-class American living with aspects of the 'super'-natural, *Poltergeist*, alongside *Close Encounters of a Third Kind* and *E.T.*, create a trilogy of films that have been defined as the Spielbergian 'Suburban Trilogy' (Gordon, 2008). Spielberg's contractual obligations with Universal surrounding the production of *E.T.* forbade him from directing another film during this work, and it has been well documented that while Spielberg was directing *E.T.* he was also producing *Poltergeist* with both films being shot nearly on the same street on location in the housing estate of Simi Valley—California (Gordon, 2008). As such, Spielberg, by taking the role of producer on *Poltergeist*, hand-picked Tobe Hooper to direct the feature—much in the same way he went onto provide Joe Dante with the directorial credit for *Gremlins* (1984).

Spielberg's ongoing themes of distrust of authority and the insertion of an external presence into the status quo as an agent of change and personal growth are present in both *E.T.* and *Poltergeist*, but the latter proves to be a far darker companion piece to the more light-hearted, upbeat alien encounter. *Poltergeist* as a film allows for the exploration of the same themes as *E.T.* but without the restrictions imposed on what was a hugely expensive, explicitly family-orientated film. Both films create a situation in which their child protagonist is put through trauma with nightmarish scenarios but while *E.T.* concludes on an ultimately uplifting finale the conclusion of *Poltergeist* by comparison is presented via a maelstrom of chaos, nihilism, and loss. This downbeat ending of *Poltergeist* also has a lot more in common with Hooper's prior work, which sees his protagonists vanquish adversity but being presented as survivors of this experience rather than the conquerors.

1.4 The duality of direction

With the film's opening in 1982 reviews, critics, and audiences not only noted the aesthetic resemblances the film shared with its 'sibling' film *E.T.* but also key narrative similarities. While both films' screenplays were derived from the same source material in *Night Skies*, *E.T.* and *Poltergeist* eventually diversified into two separate features but with both still exploring the notion of the 'super'-natural and the uncanny. Both films also provide the themes of childhood endangerment, terrorised by an external force that, ultimately through this traumatic experience, becomes a catalyst for family reconciliation. *Poltergeist*, much more so than *E.T.*, is a contradictory text, providing the viewer with the impression in its deliberate 'double ending' that the 'house is clean' when evidently this is very much not the case.

DEVIL'S ADVOCATES

As a text *Poltergeist* also presents numerous aspects of inconsistency—it is a film that is uplifting and nihilistic, genteel and horrific, and it is with these notions of duality and paradox that Spielberg and Hopper contextualise the film's narrative and direction. From the sweeping establishing shots of the new suburbs of sunny California in *Poltergeist* the viewer instantly recognises Spielbergian 'hyper-reality'. This sanitised interpretation of Americana displayed via an idyllic, white, middle-class environment framed via a perpetual carefree summer is one in which white, middle-class families live in large houses and indulge in communal white, middle-class activities and white, middle-class children safely play out. It is for these establishing shots that Spielberg is criticised in the presentation of an archetypal and unrealistic middle-class utopian fantasy (Gordon, 2008). Spielberg's drawing of the definition of a 'family' is, however, much deeper and more complex than these initial surface criticisms and critiques suggest. The families presented in *Poltergeist* and indeed *E.T.* are far more representative of a 'modern' audience of the early 1980s than the stereotypical 1950s nuclear family Spielberg is often as a director accused of idolising. While *Poltergeist* does not wholly represent or tackle head on all aspects of a dysfunctional family life, omitting aspects such as worsening economic conditions and second-wave feminism, as suggested by Nakagawa (2017), these issues are implied by Hooper and Spielberg. Both the Freelings and the Taylors (the family in *E.T.*) are presented as being argumentative, disjointed, fragmented, and far from perfect. There are of course numerous other instances of this theme of duality presented throughout the film with the juxtaposition of affection and terror in the text being an example suggested by Derry (2009), as the text shows pure unadulterated paternal love sharing space on-screen with images of the abhorrent and horrific. All these representations are framed by the presentations of thunderstorms and tornadoes outside, in turn mirroring events in the house that show the physical and emotional maelstroms that these events lead to for the family and on its environment.

Poltergeist provides two very differing creative voices within its narrative to the debates of what constitutes a representation of modern (1980s) America. For Spielberg the debates are framed by the values and lifestyle choices of the growing middle classes, overcoming adversity in both the 'super'-natural and the wider social and political context—thriving in these changes though loving solidarity. The Hooper framing, however, is one taken to represent a family who only just survive these adversities,

POLTERGEIST

Figure 1.2. Spielberg suburbia

perceiving change and modern American living as nightmarish-like. Wood (1986) states that horror is a 'collective nightmare' shared by everyone, and while Spielberg emphasises the positives Hooper seems happy to present his narrative through a nihilistic perspective, reconfiguring and annihilating any sense of returning to a status quo.

The complacency and conformity of consumerism and the bourgeois of middle-class America that are advocated by Spielberg are as such vilified by Hooper—who, while not always ruthless and cruel, does provide biting commentary on modern America through the film, specifically the bad influence that consumerism and the media has on its population. It is through this lens that Hooper's creative contribution to *Poltergeist* is evident and able to present a darker side to this idyllic suburban life. In his hands the notion of the 'American Dream' becomes an allegorical nightmare, a flimsy superficial dream built on decay and disregard of traditional values. As such, Hooper's take on this middle-class utopian fantasy is one of a lifestyle built quickly to conceal the past and its problems, built on and concreted over in a hasty attempt to move forward to fulfil sanitised consumer-driven aspirations.

DEVIL'S ADVOCATES

Hooper, in taking this perverse glee of representing this 'suburban hell' proving torment to its residents is evident, for example, in Diane's attempted escape from the back-garden swimming pool in the film's final act. The swimming pool, which initially is part of the suburban dream landscape, becomes instead a nightmare environment as the veneer of respectability is literally dug away. Her slipping and returning to the saturated, overflowing corpse-filled environment is relentless, going on longer than it should. This is a nightmare scenario drawn out to similar effect to the 'never-ending corridor' scene (which uses a contra-zoom effect to great effect to pull off an unnerving scene) as she attempts to rescue her children. This prolonged torment of his female characters is a Hooper cinematic trope, as proven in his presentation of the extended torment Sally is put through by the Sawyers in *The Texas Chain Saw Massacre*.

The film's opening shots also present Hooper's attitude towards modern-day America and his worldview of the social and political issues of the time. The first opening shot of the film is one that presents a screen full of television static, interference, and distortion. As this distortion and static eventually clear the viewer is presented with a 'close-down message' for the American broadcaster—the Star-Spangled banner ident. This visualisation can be read as Hooper's take on how television became a tool that has 'decayed' and corrupted societal norms. With the use of the environment and the objects within he deems aspects that could be framed as malignant or that provide a corruptive influence—such as television. This debate is reinforced by the presentation that while the Freeling family members are all sleeping, the television is still on—continually broadcasting its message of static and a distorted signal while nobody is even actually watching it. This argument is again reinforced as the antagonists within the film could—as ghosts—theoretically manifest anywhere (floating out of a half-dug pool, for example—as they were quite close to the surface) but instead purposefully choose the important signifier of American consumerism—the television set as a way of communicating, intruding and violating the Freeling family dynamic. While this concept of the television used as an otherworldly portal would have come directly from Spielberg's screenplay, the direction of visualising the television as a corrupting influence with the intent to distort conformity is one of Hooper trademark themes and one very much at odds when the film is being read via Spielberg's more family-thriving aspirational standpoint.

POLTERGEIST

Hooper's influence in the text can also be debated to further enhance and distil the aspects of Spielberg's 'good, modern life' and his representations of the disjointedness of the traditional modern family. Hooper's intentional distortion of the notion of a post-modern nuclear family is presented on the verge of satire, providing a wry and cutting commentary on the domestic and social decay of the 'American Dream'. While this notion was not completely lost by the late 1970s it could be argued to have become corrupted beyond recognition via the mass production of sellable aspiration to become manufactured and empty, which, in turn, reflected into the family environment and social makeup aspiring to these ideas. The sanitised and gentrified nature of Cuesta Verde, an estate full of repeated house designs set in rows of bland beige exteriors, repeated in identikit precision, all inhabited by the same socio-economic groups, is to Hooper's mind artificial, a false reality created to be a human-made environment for modern suburban living that provides little in the way of natural surroundings—a place with no personality, charm, history, or culture, again presenting modern America as one not of 'suburban heaven' but rather 'suburban hell'.

While this duality in creative outlooks encompasses the film, providing alternating perspectives of 1980s American suburban culture, some themes within the text also intersect and have inherent commonalties—the notion of distrust of authority and the ineffectuality of those meant to keep us safe from harm, for example (be that parents, authority figures, or the government). Spielberg had already presented these themes of underlying distrust towards self-appointed authority and 'experts' in both *Jaws* and in *E.T. Poltergeist* furthers these themes, presenting a narrative that shows the protagonists' willingness to ignore 'established' and pre-defined levels of authority when it comes to forces by which standard rules and traditional societal norms do not apply.

A critical retrospective of the divergent and paradoxical outlooks on the text still does not emphatically answer the question of who directed *Poltergeist* but rather presents evidence as to whose influence, style, and thematic elements were better represented within the text. Latham's (1994) opinion on the question of direction of the film suggests that the entire production of Poltergeist was an 'uneasy alliance between Spielberg's confidence in the suburban project and Hooper's corrosive contempt for bourgeois institutions' as a notion that sums up the film's conflict both on-screen and off and typifies all angles of the film's notions of duality. An example of this duality

DEVIL'S ADVOCATES

can be seen with the abduction of Carol Anne and the set-piece that 'breaks' reality and takes the narrative into the realms of the fantastical. When the supernaturally possessed tree smashes through the children's bedroom window, grabbing Robbie and attempting to consume him, one can easily imagine Spielberg, the consummate director of children, gently instructing Oliver Robbins as Robbie on how to react, while Hooper's contribution would come in the escalation of the fear and violence presented in the scene. Robbie just before this scene is 'safe' in the surroundings of his comfortable suburban house. While anxious about the growing storm outside, as he counts the seconds between lightning and thunder there is initially nothing to be fearful of. This scene typifies pure Spielbergian direction—however, it is with the arrival of the 'Other' (in the form of the possessed tree) and the move from perceived endangerment to actualised endangerment as well as the terror, viscera, and horror of the uncanny coupled with the detritus, dirt, and blood, that the influence of Hooper's directorial influences becomes evident.

As the film provides numerous sequels there is debate that while the initial fears presented in the first film are vanquished, they persist. In conjunction with the supernatural elements returning again and again in the search for Carol Anne the underlying aspects of the perceived 'horrors' of American life also still linger and are never fully defeated.

Chapter 2: The evolution of suburban horror

2.1 The 1950s through to Halloweens in Haddonfield

Genre movies, especially horror texts, have had to adapt to meet the needs of their ever-evolving and cannier audiences—with a requirement to modify and readjust contextual narratives to become more inventive when encompassing notions such as geography and location to instil a sense of fear within its viewership. Kallitsis (2018), as an example, suggests that George A. Romero's *Dawn of the Dead* (1978), by being set in a 'modern-mall', provides recognisable and familiar associations for its audience. What John Carpenter did with *The Thing* (1982) was to create an atmosphere where the environment and setting were as much part of the narrative as 'The Thing' itself.

The location and settings of horror texts need to express accessible points of identifiable cultural terms and characteristics, representative of their time to create the notion of fear in an audience (Tudor, 2002). The motif of 'invasive fear' from an unknown outside presence interjecting or corrupting the normative way of American life contextualised by a 'conservative' pre-set and pre-defined way of life has had to inherently reflect the social and political fears of the time—be that the development of atomic power, the rise of communism, or the loss of freedom or individuality. This is evident throughout the 1950s when the narrative focus of horror was expressed through invasive forces or external presences with communism thinly disguised as alien invaders encroaching on 'Main-Street USA'.

While the numerous Roger Corman and William Castle 'Attacks of' and 'Invasions of…' movies of the 1950s and 1960s took place in 'hyper-real' small town America the theme of community under siege slowly receded as the social narrative of what to 'fear' changed and audiences for these films themselves matured (both in age and cinematic sophistication). Horror narratives became more aware of the evolution and development of social change occurring in the 1960s and 1970s and an audience who were once happy to be scared by teenage werewolves now wanted to consume more socially relevant or thought-provoking texts in order to tingle their spines.

As such American horror filmmakers had to be prepared to cater to these cannier audiences wanting more sophistication in their diet of home-spun horror. The movies featuring parent-swallowing sandpits and blobs oozing from flea-pit cinemas had become as tired and clichéd as the dated representations of 'Middle America' and were slowly replaced with films set in high-rise buildings, brownstone apartments, shopping malls, and the increasingly forgotten communities left behind by social and political change. Horror as a genre came to increasingly represent the growing divides within post-war class society with films presenting other social environments that ranged from the establishment of the American gentry presented in *The Omen* (1976), to the stylised upper middle class in *Rosemary's Baby* (1968) through to the forgotten grindhouse backwaters of Texas via Tobe Hooper's *The Texas Chain Saw Massacre*.

There is a suggestion by Sharrett (2009) that the deliberate social commentary instilled in horror texts by the likes of George Romero (and indeed Tobe Hooper himself) are 'keenly critical of middle-class life and all its supporting institutions', which was at odds with those still wanting nothing more than the stylised interpretation of the '1950s nuclear family' and the 'American Dream' they were promised two decades before.

Films that were initially set within this growing suburban environment seemed at first to follow Romero in his criticism, taking the form of satirical representations of this specific lifestyle choice. The evolving pre-conceptions of social make-up, of family, and of the negative representation of the patriarch within texts such as *The Stepford Wives* (1975), based on Ira Levin's satirical novel published in 1972, for example, presented a 'hyper-realistic' interpretation of this aspiring middle-class lifestyle—contextualised via a very 1950s inspired setting that is a 'construction of a suburban landscape through the imaginary' as Rowley (2015) describes it.

Within these growing environments filmmakers could once again explore the same spaces horror narratives had left two decades earlier, now purposely presenting texts that subverted and violated these relatively new personal safe living spaces through what been described as the 'suburban horror cycle'—a thematic notion of texts that provided horror at home and could be debated to start with the release of John Carpenter's *Halloween* (1978).

POLTERGEIST

2.2 'It's a beautiful day in this neighbourhood'

By the late 1970s and the beginnings of Ronald Reagan's conservative movement (and eventual presidency) social anxiety turned to find a means to protect the American way of life of these new middle-class nuclear families from unknown dangers and potential social unrest. This need for protection was not always quantifiable (with outright nuclear war with Russia becoming unlikely) but news narratives induced suburban paranoia fed by a stream of propaganda and political rhetoric from a conservative network of media outlets reinforced that a social and life-threating threat existed (even a none-defined one) and that an unknown evil could be lurking right around every corner and signalled Americans growing alarm over 'stranger danger' (a mix of xenophobia, nationalism, and racism). Suburbia itself, however, was still a relatively new environment, lacking depth of social and communal coherence, historical context, and tradition. Heathcote (2014) states that suburbia is 'anodyne, the predictable counterpart to the unpredictable chaos of urban life'. There was still a mistrust of prefabricated living for its predictability, pre-defined, and conformed way of living—however within the context of *Poltergeist* this sense of new-ness and conformity is key in creating an effective environment of an 'inauthentic consumption centre and conformity factory' (Muzzio and Halper, 2002).

The environment of the political conservative rhetoric to incite the concept of an unknown fear as aways to retreat towards pre-conformity and 'safe' environments also harkened back to the initial fears instilled in audiences in 1950s texts where thematically genre films focused heavily on the fear of the loss of self and individuality with *Invaders from Mars* (1953) and *Invasion of the Body Snatchers* (1956) being examples of texts that presented the inherent fear of the taking away of free will. Both films were ironically remade right around the time of *Poltergeist*—the latter in 1978 and the former in 1986, directed by Tobe Hooper himself. Since Reagan idolised the 1950s his campaigning and presidency promised a return to these prosperous times and, as such, it makes sense that the themes and aetheric of the 1950s horror text would in some form make a return.

The instilled fear of losing control to an outside force or losing free will had, while being reframed for the post-war audience, still lingered in the American psyche. The media communication that ironically sold the aspiration to 'join us' in these new collective safe spaces, private estates, and gated communities to be safe from these outside forces, creating an environment that encouraged conformity, lack of individuality, and, in turn, created the loss of free will ironically created all the aspects that said audiences were fearful of.

Wood (1986) suggests that the concept of the 'Other' (the characteristics of the 'Other' being one of a state of being different from or not conforming to pre-established 'social norms' of society) once again had become internalised within America and in taking *Halloween* as a contextual baseline for the shift of horror narratives to these suburban settings The Shape (Michael Myers) can be seen as the personification of this social anxiety. He is a quintessential definition of the 'Other'—a literal faceless unknown adversary placed in an environment with the intent to alter the status quo as well as create an environment of unrest and fear. Placing this 'Other' in these new relatable suburban settings (Haddonfield—which typified 'Anywhere-USA') allowed for the development of the horror/fantasy narrative cycle of films of the early 1980s. Described as the 'suburban horror cycle' (Murphy, 2009), these films present a modernised family environment which saw narratives tackling social changes and anxieties brought about by the continuing stalemate of the Cold War, unrest in the Middle East, and the burgeoning costs to families due to the financial crisis in America at this time. Released during the mid-1980s into a media frenzy dubbed the 'Satanic Panic' (which saw the encouragement by American evangelical and conservative groups to ban film, television, and gaming that they deemed corrupting and would lead the teenage population to dabble with the occult), these films have been also described as the 'Suburban Gothic', 'Suburban Uncanny', or indeed the 'Suburban Fantastic' (McFadzean, 2017). By setting *Poltergeist* in this relatable suburban context Hooper and Spielberg initially create a 'safe' environment for the audience, one that is recognisable, homely, and welcoming. The narrative of the film, while showing trauma and tragedy (but has no death), concludes with a morality message and ending that sees a family happy reunited. When *Poltergeist* is viewed through this lens of the 'Suburban Fantastic' it is evident that Spielberg and Hooper present a text that provides numerous unnatural elements, such as a swimming pool full of skeletons, a clown with a penchant for strangulation, or a house imploding, but by setting the film in such a relatable suburban setting that viewer is more invested in the narrative, accepting these aspects of impossibility due to the very possible and relatable context. The impossible becomes more possible.

2.3 THE HAUNTING OF MODERN SUBURBIA

Cuesta Verde—the fictional estate established in *Poltergeist*—was, like a lot of post-war suburbs developed across America, based on New York's Levittown. This prototype first suburban housing development was created in Long Island from 1947 to 1951 (Muzzio & Halper, 2002), which saw the development of 2,000 homes. This initial development became the catalyst for not only social movement but, in turn, how cinema-going audiences perceived space, location, and context. There became a disassociation with the archetypal small-town America that had been present in many forms in film and television since the 1950s with audiences no longer recognising these environments, as the mass of the population (those who could afford it) moved away from these crumbling and rundown places to relocate within these growing new suburban environments.

The blandness of Cuesta Verde (translating from the Spanish for Green Slope or Hill) within *Poltergeist* is exaggerated in its intentional generic name and nature. This purposeful interchangeable suburban environment again represents the recurring theme of 'anywhere…USA', which is used by the contemporary texts of *Poltergeist*, debatably fetishising the obsession and attempt to return to 1950s Americana (Brehmer, 2018), overlaying this notion with the attributes of consumerism. *A Nightmare on Elm Street* (1984), for example, is set in Springwood, *Gremlins* (1984) is set in Kingston Falls, and *Back to the Future* (1985) takes place in Hill Valley, all of which are purposely interchangeable suburban environments with identikit strip malls, shopping centres, and suburban housing estates. Murphy (2009) suggests that these suburban horror narratives tap into the fear of this suburban space, creating a blank environment purposefully designed towards conformity in which to untether the uncanny. Kellner (1983a) notes, '[W]ho would want to watch a drama of a family losing job, home, and then being torn apart, an event which has become all too familiar during the past decade of permanent economic crisis?' but the popularity of these texts during these times ironically proves that this is exactly what audiences at the time wanted to consume.

Within *Poltergeist* Spielberg and Hooper utilise the location of Agoura Hills/Forest Hill to create the environment of the suburban uncanny. Situated in Simi Valley in North Los Angeles this vast new housing estate was perfectly genetic and, as Subissati (2010)

DEVIL'S ADVOCATES

describes, is a development that can be seen that cannibalised the landscape, essentially consuming the open natural space of California. In an online article Zakarin, quoting Spencer (2015), states that even the Freeling house in which the film is set was picked for its normality and conformity:

> Steven liked that house because it was the end of the road…was a two storey Valley-type mock Tudor and it just fit everything. The neighbourhood [was what] we call 'Spielbergia,' where *E.T.* and a couple of his other films were shot. He always wanted to be in normal residential areas.

The house used within the film was intentionally picked for its normality—to be unambiguous and not to stand out from the rest of the prefabrication and endless repetition of the estate. By its having no discernible identity, Spielberg and Hooper emphasise the soulless and clinical nature of the wider suburban sprawl which encroached upon and devoured small-town America. As such, the purposely aesthetically generic and emotionally barren suburban sprawl, in which nobody wants to stand out, codes the house, street, and vast suburban estate as a place to be desired by those looking to insulate themselves and their family from everyone and, indeed, everything else happening in a wider social, political, and economic context.

These purposefully blank environments as such created fertile hunting grounds for silent killers, bladed gloved demons, and restless spirits with filmmakers such as Wes Craven, Tom Holland, and Joe Dante fully exploiting these spaces to create new places in which the horror icons of the 1980s could fester. *Poltergeist*, being released at the beginning of this movement in 1982, can be debated to be one of the first texts to embrace these new vague yet relatable environments and to be one of the texts that assisted in bridging the gap between 'R' rated films and the more family-friendly/teen-focused horror pictures that followed, bringing horror into the mainstream.

Murphy's (2009) debates on the 'suburban gothic' explains that there is an 'apparent disparity between the outwardly placed, banal exterior of the modern suburban home and the sheer incongruity therein of any overtly supernatural incident'. Cuesta Verde is portrayed as perfectly 'safe'—diametrically opposed, for example, to the back roads of Texas, the roadside Funhouses, or downtown streets of Los Angeles of Hooper's prior films. As such when the text proceeds in its narrative to present elements of the

POLTERGEIST

Figure 2.1. Housing estate

impossible or uncanny to the viewer the impact is significantly amplified. The presentation of this safe space makes every aspect of external violation and chaos by the 'Other' (in the case of *Poltergeist* this 'Other' being presented as 'The Beast') feel more impactful as it intervenes with the 'perfect' order of the family structure of the Freelings.

This depiction of a safe suburbia setting with uncanny qualities is mirrored within *E.T.*; however, *Poltergeist*'s representation of these very same spaces and environment is not one of a benevolent intrusion within a perfect family environment but rather one of an aggressive force 'punching' its way into the stiflingly oppressive and conforming nature of suburbia. There is significant emphasis (especially within the trailer for the film) that the houses, streets, and estate all look the same and are unnaturally ordered and conformed to near uncanny perfection as the epitome of 'packaged suburbia' (Kellner, 1983a), and with this emphasis on order and structure the protagonist (The Beast) is much more aggressive in its violation of these spaces. We see physical objects tearing the family apart, and familial bonds bringing it back together. The family dynamic is therefore threatened by the objects that it supposedly needs for perfection and comfort in post-war America.

While the same estate is used by both texts with near duplicate roads, houses, and setting providing the environment for the narrative of both films the representation of Cuesta Verde in *Poltergeist* provides a greater emphasis on isolation than community.

25

Michelson (2018) states that the emphasis on self-imposed order and purposely chosen closed environments is to 'create an atmosphere of artificial perfection'. While the trappings of suburban lifestyle are evident, the houses on the estate are insular—with the emphasis on personal space, be that of the family unit or an individual within this home space. The house, gardens, and front lawns are all designed to be living spaces but at the same time these spaces are intended not to be shared—you may well live near your neighbours, but you will never really get to know them. This disassociation even with such geographical closeness and proximity is evident within the narrative when Steven and Diane ask their neighbours for help but are left in the doorway to get bitten by mosquitoes.

Poltergeist pitches this pre-designed (manufactured) impersonal environment, emphasising issues such as the lack of sense of community and shared experience—an environment that seems content to cover up its flaws (Morton, 2016). While the houses are lined up this is not an environment conducive to making connections with others, and as Harry Medved within his text *Location Filming in Los Angeles* (2010) states:

> The movie made the area look like it was over-developed. But in actuality, it's a beautiful bedroom community surrounded by rolling hills, dozens of hiking trails, parks, and playgrounds and hundreds of historic oak trees…With all the surrounding green space, you wouldn't recognize it from *Poltergeist*'s establishing shots.

As a text *Poltergeist* can be recognised as building the foundations for the 'haunted suburbia' sub-genre influencing not only its own filmmaking contemporaries but also current and modern and texts. New lifestyles' choices, aspirations, and altering political views became the discursive points on which to build new contexts of horror narratives. The settings of suburbia, large homes, and luxury goods and the coding of a confirmative 'happy family' represent the Baby Boomer generation coming to maturity. These representations of the modern progressively replace the establishment hierarchies, tropes, and settings of the supernatural and gothic; these traditions are instead superseded by what has been described as the 'technical uncanny' (Bassett, 2020), in which the modern environment makes itself strange to us. Director James Wan is noted for saying, 'Poltergeist scarred me for life' (cited in Lee, 2016) in highlighting the film's influences on his own work, which situates supernatural phenomena in ordinary

POLTERGEIST

and/or relatively new environments such as *Insidious* (2010) and *The Conjuring* (2013). These use similar contexts and environments that Hooper and Spielberg established to shape new experience, much in the same way they themselves used *The Haunting* (1963) as a source of inspiration.

2.4 ENVIRONMENT AS THE ENEMY

The environments and battlegrounds of horror in the early 1980s by moving into these suburban spaces presented film that not only focused on the subjugation, domination, and possession of the feminine but instead with films like *The Amityville Horror* (1979) and *Poltergeist* had the antagonists attack every individual within the family via the spaces in which these individuals dwell (Grant, 1996). The setting of *Poltergeist* in an ultra-modern family home, full of televisions and assorted paraphernalia replaces the more traditional environments of horror narratives. These archetypical horror spaces had become as much of a cliché as the Counts and mad scientists who had inhabited them. Films such as *Carry on Screaming!* (1966), *Young Frankenstein* (1974), *The Rocky Horror Picture Show* (1975), and even *The Man with Two Brains* (1983) all parodied these tropes and traditions, reframing what had once been deemed to be frightening and had 'domesticated of the Gothic' according to Mulvey-Roberts (1998).

In *Poltergeist*, the audience sees the Freeling family within their ultra-modern living spaces, surrounded by everything the suburban family could ever desire, with hallmarks of wealth such as a new swimming pool, an abundance of toys, and comforts for the children (as well as wry nods to other genre references, such as Incredible Hulk toys, *Star Wars*' (1977) memorabilia, and an *Alien* (1979) poster on the wall in Carol Anne and Robbie's room), being deliberate choices to create, as Schneider (1999) notes while citing Jentsch, the feeling that 'we should not be frightened here'. As such, when the intrusion into this space and environment by the uncanny occur the home is no longer presented to be a safe space. The comfortable surroundings of the house through the text are transformed to become one of a prison in which the inhabitants are trapped and the consumer goods within it are turned into weapons. The house becomes an opposing space, confining the family within its walls—there is no need for barren moors, isolated castles, or impenetrable locations when the family are restrained and confined

27

by the very nature of their environment. They live but only metres away from their neighbours, but social conformity and their uncanny circumstances do not allow them to call for help from them. With Carol Anne's disappearance the family turn inward with the plight taking place behind their closed doors, the scenario and family home now deemed to be shameful and monstrous. The once nurturing space of the family home eventually becomes 'unhomely' (a more precise translation of the German word 'unheimlich' from which the term 'uncanny' was originally derived). Chaston (1997), citing Stephen King in his work *Danse Macabre* (1983), comments on home as negative space, calling it 'the archetype of the Bad Place' that, through the narratives, degrades to become a contaminated space with the home environment becoming un-liveable and unlinked with the family. Through this forced entrapment process the viewer sees the morality at the core of the narrative, which highlights the importance of love and family over consumerism and wastefulness. The rescuing of Carol Anne from the 'Other Side' frees the family from their own house-bound entrapment, that being both the physical entrapment and the consumer-driven mind-set. However, the family's reward for being reunited and escaping the confines of conformity comes with the literal removal of all their worldly goods as the house implodes at the climax of the film.

Barthes (2009) calls this narrative phenomenon 'inoculation'—a local event that personifies and identifies a specific evil to divert attention away from fundamental and underlying malignant wider social issues. This theory suggests that it is not what is under the house that is the antagonist for the text but rather the initial mind-set and motivational factors of the family and wider social themes of greed and consumption. The Freelings are seen to learn that the pursuit of these goals in the taking of the house and the removal of all material goods could be seen to resolve the family of any and all responsibility for the horror—they are left with nothing, an apt punishment, and penance for transgressions of the 'greed is good' mentality. By being left with no consumer trappings they (to use a modern term) become 'woken', finding the error of their ways in their pursuit of consumerism.

This progression of the narrative towards the eventual resolution that evidences the growth of a family unit can be read in two separate ways. Both would suggest the necessity that the insertion of the 'Uncanny' or 'Other' as a force to bring about change is needed. From a 'Spielbergian' perspective the film's resolution comes from the continued assault on the traditional way of family life, bringing trauma to effect change before the resolution and eventual new, similar status quo is established. Viewed through the perspective of a 'Hooper-esque' lens the 'Other' as an invasive chaotic element is never resolved and the conflict and trauma become part of the institutions of family, establishing the new status quo to be one of potential continued conflict (and the inevitable sequel).

2.5 BURYING THE PAST

The contemporaries of *Poltergeist* defined within the 1980s 'haunted suburbia' texts illustrate the cost of the push for modernity so often associated with the growth of suburban gentrification and the purist of consumerism for deeper wants and desires. The thematic importance of the setting and environment of *Poltergeist*, wrapped as it is in the 'newness' of suburban America and the consumer-driven concepts that underpin the American Dream, is to do with the process and drive of making profit and surface-level consumerism of goods as the divisive factor within the text. There is little respect for tradition; scratch the surface and it is evident that the lifestyle and way of living of that generation was built on trauma and enslavement.

Poltergeist revisits the clichéd 'Native American burial ground' trope that had become familiar with viewers, having appeared in *The Amityville Horror* as well as other screenplays and novels. *Poltergeist*'s narrative can be read as a case of 'cosmic justice'— in which those involved with Westernised invasive suburban growth, disrespect for traditions, and lack of respect for the dead see those disturbed rise and are punished for their transgressions. The narrative's conclusion is unable to find resolution until the physical objects of domination—that is, the suburban home itself and everything within it—are destroyed.

There are numerous examples within *Poltergeist* of disregard for what is perceived to be old, out of date, or unwanted. No sooner as Carol Anne's bird Tweety is found lying on its back dead with no pause for remorse she states, 'Can I have a goldfish now?'—which, of course, she gets. Specific images and visuals presented in *Poltergeist*, as also evident within *The Texas Chain Saw Massacre*, highlight the notion that the world has grown disordered and unnatural, under a 'malefic influence' presenting the world that is turned upside down—evident in a literal sense during the scene in which Diane is attacked by the poltergeists and pushed unnaturally up the wall and onto the ceiling of the family home. Taking this debate further the notion of inversion is present within *The Texas Chain Saw Massacre* where the viewer is presented with an upturned dead armadillo, a scene comparable to the one in *Poltergeist* again involving Tweety in which the bird's corpse is shown above the grave rather than buried within it—spilling open when dug up. This returning to the surface and presenting the dead is also prevalent in the film's finale when the corpses appear in the swimming pool and those buried under the house burst through the floor as a way again of highlighting the upturning of perceived normalcy.

Hooper had already tackled the thematic trend of 'newness' and the contemporary hurriedly replacing the old within *The Texas Chain Saw Massacre*, suggesting that the old America 'traditions' such as butchery as a 'family business', skills passed down from father to son, and generations of workers within a family who have been working in the same role (factory, funhouse, or abattoir) were becoming redundant, easily replaced, and forgotten as the move towards technological improvements, autonomous processes, and the growing of profits though capitalism dominated entire industries (Guillory, 2002).

This is shown repeatedly throughout *Poltergeist*—the affluence, wastefulness, and lack of appreciation of 'things' and material goods by a generation brought up content, middle class, and wanting for nothing with the abandoned children's bikes, the excesses of food at the breakfast table, and the toys and consumables scattered through the house show a disregard for order and where with the quick and ease of consumerism things are not seen as precious and very much as disposable. The literal 'history' and soul of America within the text is being built over and replaced with the pursuit of new wants, desires, and aspirations driven by and catered to by soul-less companies. The motifs of burying the past or building over are strongly connected to the suburban lifestyle and its elements of gentrification and modern 'mod-con' or convenience living.

When Mr Teague and Steve Freeling walk across the hill at the top of the valley looking down on Cuesta Verde the scene is filled with meaning of the toxicity to achieve the idyllic suburban dream promised in the 1950s to the population of America. Initially the

POLTERGEIST

walk is past the white picket fences—one of the symbols that defined this dream. As the walk continues, however, it is revealed that the fence becomes decayed and in ill repair and is there to represent the boundaries of a graveyard—a wry nod by Hooper on the continued thematic elements of the past being buried but at the same time ready to encroach on the 'living' world.

Figure 2.2. Estate overview

While the graves themselves are passive, a symbol of the sacrifices, context, and history of America that the narrative blatantly chooses to ignore, they act as a catalyst for the corruption and decay they represent. There is nothing malevolent about leaving the dead alone to rest—the horror in the narrative comes not from the bodies laid at rest below the surface, but rather from the way in which the living, especially those focused on the material rather than the spiritual, purposely choose to ignore the dead and their history and desecrate that which came before them. This act of desecration is a catalyst for the event, in that by removing the headstones and not the bodies, the developers have disrupted the bonds between the living beings of the present and the deceased generations of the past; as Beauregard (2006) notes, 'It is as if Americans have struck a Faustian bargain in which progress has been traded for self-reflection, compassion, and a sense of history.'

This presentation of surface tension and the decay of the 'old' just lying underneath the thin veneer of respectability all too ready to overflow into the new is a key point of the text—from the physical cutting of the earth for the swimming pool to the literal dead rising from the ground, to the poltergeists 'punching' through to this reality, and the breach between the spirit world and ours through Carol Anne's closet the text provided numerous examples of the breach between the natural/unnatural, old/new, and the physical and the spiritual.

These dichotomies resolved through interjection could be debated to appear due to the lack of established American cultural history (excluding Native American traditions) and the speed in which there is an attempt to establish this. With the country only existing for just over two hundred years there is a debate that culturally America has had no time to propagate its own 'mythology' and narrative tradition and the only way to establish this is to build and rebuild, covering what has come before to establish something new. 'Americans' as a collective culture is based on mass immigration and, as such, had to recycle and indeed re-appropriate from other older, more established cultures from where families and individuals originated. This highlighting of America's lack of cultural history is evident in contemporary texts such as Neil Gaiman's *American Gods* (2001), which suggest that America is worshipping 'new gods' (television, mass communication, and media) that have replaced the 'old gods' and traditions, but these 'new gods' can themselves be presented as equally mean or spiteful or fear inducing as any prior deity.

CHAPTER 3: TRICKSTERS AND FAIRY TALES

Poltergeist, like its counterpart *E.T.*, presents an exploration of childhood fantasies, a modernised fairy tale that unlike the more uplifting (and yet still surprisingly dark) extra-terrestrial narrative pushes the boundaries of the 'Suburban Fantastic' (McFadzean, 2019) to its extremes, distorting the context of suburban family melodrama into one of horrific fantasy.

With *Poltergeist* Hooper and Spielberg attempted to remove the environment and setting that pre-defined traditional gothic horror signifiers, replacing them instead with the trappings of contemporary 1980s American suburbia. With this updating of place and environment *Poltergeist* has provided differing debates, commentary, and analysis within the realms of horror studies, specifically in the context of social studies and American politics of the late 1970s and 1980s. The discursive point relevant to *Poltergeist* is also the relative newness of the developing middle classes in America, portrayed in this film to be one often defined by their overt consumerism and indulgent home comforts, issues that reinforce critical commentary and debate surrounding the perceived lack of maturity of 'white Anglo-Saxon' American traditions, culture, history, and mythology.

Poltergeist, for all its social and political commentary on modern living, sunshine, and suburbia, is still very much reliant on the need to scare (it is a horror film after all) and framing the film within the context of the lack of American 'mythology' must rely more on traditional folklore motifs and fairy-tale storytelling traditions to underpin its modern narrative setting. The plot takes and utilises direct influences from other more mature cultures, delving into a shared public domain of myths, lore, and traditions to instil and present the film's universal motifs of primal motifs of fears. The agencies of change that underpin the film's narrative include the interjection of aggressive external forces into a community/ family, an inherent fear of the dead, the loss of an offspring, and the lack/ impotence of personal control of a situation, which are all 'traditional' storytelling tropes and motifs. The opposition and agency of the 'hero' to rally against these situations are also present within *Poltergeist* and as such it provides in the narrative a very Campbellian 'Hero's Journey' with framing as a modern interpretation but based on the traditions of hereditary storytelling.

DEVIL'S ADVOCATES

While the surroundings and 'world-building' of the screenplay of *Poltergeist* represents the new and modern with the manifestation of the monstrous presented within the texts (by the award-winning visual and optical effects team) still very much established are traditional folkloric tropes and conventions. It is the application and use of natural phenomena (storms), aggressive and dangerous environments (trees and mud) and the unclean, unhealthy, or unnatural (the dead rising) that are utilised to induce fear. *Poltergeist* presents this array of collective horror triggers as well as utilising more 'extreme' taboos such as self-mutilation, child endangerment, and attempted sexual assault into the narrative to further enhance the notions relating to anxiety and fear.

The text also provokes emotive fear within its audience from things we cannot perceive in the material world—a realm of the 'spiritual' or 'afterlife' defined in the text as 'the other side'. This fear of the unknown, the 'super'-natural, and of realms beyond our current understanding underpin other primal fears of the viewer's perceptions and understanding. The protagonists have no comprehension or perception of their predicament, moving as they do from a 'natural' family life to one which confronts a realm of the 'unnatural', filled with spirits, monsters, and the 'afterlife'; the eventual traversal to this place of 'the other side' creates a narrative in which the protagonists venture into the unknown. The definitions set out in Joseph Campbell's 'Hero's Journey' monomyth state that a story's protagonists need to traverse into a special world. This space could be, for example, an aggressive environment of natural phenomena (storms and lightning, for instance) or, indeed, a spiritual realm of the 'other side'—both of which are present within the text. The narrative 'story' or journey cycle which the Freeling family endure sees them in the same position as their heroic predecessors in having to cross a threshold and venture into this special world, well beyond the limits of their own understanding of this unknown. By the crossing of this threshold from the ordinary environment into the extra-ordinary, the film's narrative shifts, mirroring the viewer's trepidation as they are purposefully led into this 'unknown' and, as such, creating an environment purposely designed to incite fear.

With the text the showing of the horror of the ordeal is defined successfully through the lens of childhood fears by presenting these unnatural storms, monstrous trees, gaping mouths, skeletal creatures, and grasping tendrils through the perceptions of Carol Anne and Robbie. By doing this, these monstrous images and scenarios are emphasised to an even greater extent, distilled and focused by a child's lack of understanding or comprehension. While the events of the film are not fully understood by the mature participants these nightmarish images, which are found to mirror a lot of 'Grimm' fairy tales, traditional storytelling, and mythological canon induce fear to an even greater extent when there is a lack of rational thinking and imaginative and childlike perception involved.

While the instillation of unnerving images and situations to provoke fear is contextually updated to induce a response from a modern and 'canny' audience, the underlying human nature, which is wary of the unseen or unknown, is still a primal instinct and is present within the film. The things that will cause us harm, the monsters and unseen creatures that lurk, are now under the bed or in the wardrobe rather than in darkened woods or hidden in the night; the fear of the unseen and unknown still triggers the fight/flight instincts. Our sense of pareidolia (seeing faces in inanimate objects, such as the crack in the wall or in the shadows) occurs for a reason, and with the contextualisation and transposition of these primal fears into a familiar, safe setting of family life, the nightmarish quality of the film is enhanced significantly.

Spielberg and Hooper's vivisection of a traditional modern family of 'perfected' middle-class lifestyle provides a convincing fictional case study into the trauma of the loss of a child though the use of a supernatural framing device. A fully relatable emotional spectrum of fear, loss, and anger as well as the physical portrayal of the stresses, compassion, and final relief of reunion are wholly evident within the film's run time, and while the text is reviewed and critiqued as a fantasy/horror tale or modern fairy story Spielberg, for all his perceived niceties, Americanised 'kitsch', and overt family melodrama in his early cinematic works does overall provide a terrifying tale that shows off his obvious fascination with mythology and the supernatural. This exploration into the realms of the fantastic are underpinned with a maturity and darkness that was present even within his initial draft of this film, which was entitled *Night-Terrors*, an apt name for a film that brings primordial terrors and the fear of the unknown into the sunshine setting of modern-day America.

DEVIL'S ADVOCATES

3.1 THE INVOKING OF SPIRITS

With the uttering of the subsequently ubiquitous and highly recognisable tag line of the film, 'They're here', Carol Anne verbalises the arrival of the 'Other' into the narrative of the film. This 'Other' does indeed conform to traditional sociology and critical theory readings and interpretations of otherness in its constructs of identity. This presentation of the 'Other' within the film is presented as invasive unworldly external presence, especially to the established social category of the Freelings who are coded very much as the typical white, suburban, middle-class family.

The depersonalisation of the film's antagonists as 'They' also reaffirms the aspect of something that cannot be categorised, defined, or interpreted. The coding of the poltergeists as a 'They' as a non-specific pronoun mirrors the inability of the protagonists of the film to describe or verbalise who and what is happening to them, instilling the deep-rooted childhood fear of having no control, agency, or authority of a situation. In uttering this oft-repeated catchphrase these two relatively harmless words prove a simple but effective foreshadowing technique for the narrative.

Poltergeists as antagonists has not commonly been utilised within the traditional horror canon with their ethereal nature being very much at odds with the more physical manifestations. While creature-feature horror texts throughout film history have presented a wide range of recognisable 'monsters', such as zombies, mummies, or aliens, the antagonists within *Poltergeist* were not so easily identifiable.

Prior horror texts had provided ghost stories and spirits on-screen for decades— from adaptations of M.R. James's early twentieth-century ghost stories through to the 1980s *The Changeling* to various presentations of *A Christmas Carol*, cinema had already portrayed ghosts and spirits countless times building on pre-existing mythologies or definitions from either prior cinematic outings or literature. Poltergeists, however, had a lack of recognition and pre-established definition for audiences to identify with and while news at the time presented 'real' events such as the 'Enfield Poltergeist' creating a new mythology for a new horror antagonist became an interesting conundrum for the filmmakers to portray.

While *The Amityville Horror* and other texts had presented 'angry spirits' via the reconfiguring of the haunted house motif to a modernised suburban setting a brand new-build house was not something audiences had seen before. As such, the film in presenting something completely new meant there was no pre-defined management of expectation and no set 'rules' to have to adhere to—as such the question raised was what a poltergeist could and could not do. This ambiguity allowed for a new 'canon' and creative freedom to be built for the filmmakers without the restrictions and limitations of pre-set horror 'lore' and allowed for the presentation of an antagonist for which they themselves could set the 'rules', which could be adjusted accordingly for the needs of the narrative.

This uniqueness and purposeful ambiguity of the poltergeists' existence creates a situation within the narrative by which the protagonists and authorities are hard pressed to counteract the 'unknown' malevolence with known cultural methods (crosses, garlic, silver bullets, or a more obscure MacGuffin such as a Proton Pack) and, as such, a more fantastical, unconventional solution must be found to counteract the antagonists in the form of medium and psychic Tangina Barrons. By humanising the rally against an inhuman force, the narrative allows for the thematic elements of the importance of family, love, and the humanity of the character's journey to become a central aspect of the film. By focusing on the human drama the text provides numerous relatable examples of characters' physical, emotional, and personal trauma framed in a wider social and economic landscape by the threat of loss of power and authority.

The emphasis on the lack of definition as to what 'they' are and the purposefully ill-defined nature of the poltergeists seemed intentional on the part of the screen-writers, allowing for considerably more scope in imagination and visualisation, which was brought to life through optical effects, practical effects, and camera trickery by the award-winning visual effects team who created iconic set pieces within the film and allowed Spielberg to construct his own interpretation of the intrusive supernatural presence terrorising the family. Poltergeists provided something new, innovative, and visually spectacular that fully embraced the innovations made during the late 1970s within optical and visual effects by companies such as Industrial Light and Magic. This purposeful disregard for convention allowed for the presentation of the film's unpredictable set pieces and is used to great effect by the film's dual climaxes and eventual resolution.

3.2 VISIONS OF EXCESS

The presentation of the unknown and an unrecognisable antagonist allowed the filmmakers to generate a greater sense of unease to present a film that played on the abhorrent, traditional jump-scares. and childhood fears presented via stunning practical visual effects sequences to iconic effect. Set pieces such as the depiction of near drowning in a filthy pool of decaying dead bodies to the visceral horror of a character tearing off his own face are key moments that define the film visually and narratively. Even the execution and direction of the screenplay turns a potentially absurd notion of a supernatural anthropomorphic tree that eats children into something that is raw, unflinching, and visually shocking. In the presentation of these visceral images (and more) *Poltergeist* is not subtle in its execution—the decaying corpses, apparitions, and gaping maws are not just horrific in nature to create instant revulsion for the sake of a cheap jump scare; the 'horror' of the set pieces while pronounced and explicit (utilising practical effects to their fullest extent) are designed to be as nightmarish as possible to underpin the film's themes of much deeper trauma.

These explorations of the concept of loss, on both physical and emotional levels, is one of the key underlying themes of the film. The physical removal of a child from a family environment (whether they have been eaten by a tree, transported through the closet to the other side of the television screen, or simply abducted) and eventual loss of the Freelings's worldly possessions prove to be terrifyingly 'real' and relatable representations of trauma and fear. *Poltergeist's* successful presentation of these relatable aspects of human suffering and trauma blended with more fantastical elements provide the film with layered representations of fear, while being submerged in a swimming pool full of skeletons or being confronted by vast ghostly apparitions from a closet are instantaneously 'scary' but the underlying trauma of child engagement, loss or removal of personal power are far more emotively abhorrent and repugnant than the numerous creatures depicted on screen.

3.3 TRICKSTERS

Lewis Spence's *Encyclopaedia of Occultism* (2006) defines a poltergeist as a 'noisy spirit'—a supernatural entity whose traits are ones that are 'immature' or 'brattish'. This

POLTERGEIST

defined trait of playfulness and child-like interaction is established early in the film with the main antagonists depicted as playful, as the initial manifestations of the poltergeists are performed for attention-seeking reasons—none-threatening pranks and phenomena presented in a similar manner to a child attempting to gain a parent's attention.

The 'Ask Dad' scene in the film is where all the children are at a breakfast table attempting to attain agency and authority as they talk across one another with each individual attempting to be heard while at the same time taunting and mimicking the others. This realistic way of children attempting to attain attention and organically getting louder and more boisterous escalates eventually to the point where the poltergeists interject, joining in the Freeling children's unruly behaviour by taking the proceeding a step 'too far', initially bending the cutlery and then not wanting the other children to drink milk by shattering their drinking glasses (milk being seen as 'good' for children, and therefore it standing to reason for it to be spilt by naughty children). The pushing by children at boundaries of acceptable behaviour while in turn also testing authority figures mirror real child psychology where the over-zealous actions and externalised expressions of ill-behaviour are represented in children where contact, support, and emotional dependence are desired (Gewirtz, 1956).

Figure 3.1. Ask Dad

DEVIL'S ADVOCATES

The initial representation and interaction with the poltergeists as initially playful unseen forces provided an intriguing introduction to the antagonists of the film. While a physical manifestation of the spirits had already been seen and a communication and initial link with Carol Anne already established the slow coercion and encouragement to 'play' by the antagonists within the film is a sly, manipulative, and intelligent way of getting the family to accept and welcome the 'Other' into the family environment. Representations of ghosts in other films such as *Full Circle* (1977), *The Sentinel* (1977), *The Amityville Horror* and *The Entity* are all represented as using force and aggression to attain their goals; even the representation of more 'benevolent' ghosts such as Joseph Carmichael in *The Changeling* are also shown to using forceful methods to gain attention and action.

Within *Poltergeist*, the family, while initially portrayed as confused by the ghostly occurrences (unknowing that is what the phenomenon is), are not presented as being panicked or fearful; the spirits make it 'fun' to interact, piquing interest by presenting a playable game (of moving across the floor) to baffle and bemuse, using subterfuge with the intention of slowly coercing the Freelings to let their guard down and accept this strange yet benevolent scenario—an act that succeeds as Diane is enthralled when she finds that she can play with the apparitions, not knowing what the unexplained occurrence is and treating the occurrence as a novelty or bizarre curio rather than anything malevolent.

The ghosts are coded as naughty children, defining the actions of the antagonists as puerile and purposeful, providing an open display of mischievous and destructive tendencies. When Doctor Lesh and the team enter Carol Anne's bedroom, the ghosts mock and laugh while levitating the toys, and the demeanour of the 'child-spirits' changes from playfulness and 'showing off' to becoming more confrontational. This enthusiasm for aggressive, child-like, and anti-establishment behaviour is evident from moving Carol Anne's bed across the spinning room into a vortex and even having the toy of the Hulk ride a horse and playing the record with a protractor, which are all childlike in their acts. This bringing in of Doctor Lesh and her team changes the dynamic with the family going outside of their material unit for assistance. In bringing in an outside element to provide authority in the person of Doctor Lesh, whose authority is framed as that of a teacher, she wields authority, power, and knowledge and is there to oversee and inspect and as well, if needed, provide discipline. As such, the actions the poltergeists exhibit devolve

POLTERGEIST

into worse behaviour with actions becoming more ill-tempered, aggressive, and angry, mirroring a child who pushes back when confronted with authority and as a result being told off or disciplined. The spirits also seem to mock and to become purposely confrontational, pointing a spike of a compass at Doctor Lesh at the door or the small wind-up robot letting out a high hysterical giggle at Robbie. The poltergeists also begin to show off their prowess and powers in more volatile ways, such as the repeated use of biting, an action again taken by children when they become aggressive, angry, or are confronted by authority.

Every encounter with the spirts at this juncture of the film presents evidence of immature aggression and childlike behaviour from the antagonists. Authority and disciple has been needed as they have been 'naughty' and as such been 'sent to their room'—a space that they now occupy and are confrontational about, not wanting others to occupy it (essentially a supernatural 'get out of my room' scenario). An example of which can be seen when Diane in a quiet moment tries to open the door to Carol Anne's room by herself and receives a loud angry scream projected at her when she tries to enter the space.

These actions of playfulness evolving through to eventual aggression of the poltergeists themselves mirror recognised commonalities, tropes, and traditions found within various national folklore. The initially child-like playfulness of the 'Other'—that which is previewed as different and categorised with an unknown quality—turning into malevolence is a common trope within literature as too are the representations of spirits intent on child abductions that use guile and trickery rather than force in their actions. The poltergeists within the film are presented to be more akin to the characters and legends such as changelings, fairies, or the little folk found within Norse/Celtic/Germanic mythologies as well as mirroring stories such as *Rattenfänger von Hameln* (the Pied Piper) and the works collated by the Brothers Grimm or taken directly from traditional Western fairy tales.

Due to its relatively short existence as a nation, modern America is not overly abundant with folklore or mythology (defining of course 'modern American' as to not include traditional native American cultures), however the storytellers, writers, and modern myth-makers of the US have produced an abundance of modern American contemporary cultural signifiers that can be defined under the concept of 'spectral

America' (Blanco and Peeran, 2013), giving readers numerous modern representations of ghosts, spirts, and the uncanny across the spectrum of twentieth-century media (written works of news and prose, radio, television and film).

As *Poltergeist* is contextualised as a modern take on a traditional horror narrative the poltergeists are presented as updated 'tricksters' immersing themselves within the surroundings they inhabit—hiding and 'glamouring' themselves into the trappings of modern suburban living. Rather than roaming the haunted castles and ancient forests to trap the unwary, Spielberg's screenplay presents the agitated spirts as adapting to the environment, applying new takes on old traditions—gone are the haunted paintings, replaced instead with possessed familiar household objects, and the magic mirrors, crystal balls, and enchanted reflections replaced instead by television screens and fluorescent-lit bathroom mirrors and half-dug swimming pools.

The high-end, modern living accompaniments of the Freeling home presented by the abundance of televisions, toys, and material goods are also a modern representation of wealth and status; again gone is the fairy-tale finery presented in castles or balls, replaced by social gatherings to watch football matches on television. This 'enchantment through wealth' motif has also been modernised with magic spinning wheels, spells, and magic being replaced by the new 'glamour' sold via advertising and the consumer culture. This modernising of conventional story tropes re-appropriates and reinterprets traditions and mythologies, providing a way to link to a past that again highlights the point that contextually Westernised American cultural mythology lacks depth.

The film portrayal of the antagonists has them using traits commonly associated with folkloric trickster characters within storytelling such as the Coyote, Br'er Rabbit, or Loki, using disguise or beguilement to seduce or corrupt. This utilisation of trickery is applied to great effect by the spirits in *Poltergeist* in their abduction of Carol Anne. Within the text Tangina states as a matter of fact that the main antagonist of the film, 'The Beast', lies to Carol Anne while she is on the 'Other Side', noting that he (or it) takes the form of another child, telling her things that only children know. This seduction and outright lying by a corruptive presence pretending to be something it is not is comparable to representations in literature of 'evil' corrupting the innocent. In presenting and framing the film's antagonists as these liars, unruly deceivers, or as agents for chaos the poltergeists in the film can be defined also as traditional theatrical pranksters. The

POLTERGEIST

portrayals of 'The Fool' as a disruptive element of the narrative dates to classical Greek theatre where there are characters such as 'sklêro-paiktês' that are associated with the elements of 'play' and whose child-like qualities on stage are there to create upheaval and chaos. Additionally, the notion of a devil or demon whispering in the ear of the virtuous, saintly, or virginal 'hero' is presented many times in medieval paintings, poems, and literature and, as Tangina again notes, the corruption and beguilement aimed towards Carol Anne works, stating, 'To her, it is simply another child…to us it is The Beast.'

While *Poltergeist* reframes traditional Western fairy tales, myths, and legends in their representations of 'Otherness' to a modern audience, having the spirits framed as modernised or contemporary tricksters that use slyness and guile to achieve their goals and the antagonists as fools or pranksters could be debated to be deliberate. The alignment of the film's antagonists to be representations of phantom Harlequins or supernatural jesters invokes a highly modernised physical representation of 'Otherness' and presents one of the most significant and iconic motifs associated with the film—that of the visualisation of the clown.

3.4 BRING ON THE CLOWNS

It would be difficult to discuss at any length *Poltergeist*'s contribution to the lexicon of modern-day cinematic horror iconography without discussing the film's significant contribution to the growth of coulrophobia—the inherent fear of clowns.

While clowns were typically perceived to be 'fools', written, scripted, or portrayed as characters to entertain or amuse, the traditional semiotics of the 'folly', which includes made-up painted faces, silks, and colourful dress (red noses, vivid wigs, and enlarged hands and feet came later) have become signifiers that have become transmuted from something light-hearted and comedic into something that has connotations and association with the fearful or horrific.

The loss or distortion of a performer's recognisable facial features by covering them with make-up creates a character or persona that, while being recognisable, is also at the same time unrecognisable. A clown's iconography of bizarre or colourful outfits, exaggerated movements, and actions that are 'child-like' but performed by an adult

43

(McAndrew, 2016) can very much be framed in the context of the 'Uncanny Valley'—the representation of a human being that is 'almost' like us, but not (Bala, 2013).

Alongside Pennywise from *IT* (1989) and other 1980s horror texts such as *The House on Sorority Row* (1983), *Ghoulies* (1985), and *Killer Klowns from Outer Space* (1988) mirroring real-world trauma perpetrated by the like's serial killer John Wayne Gacy, the image of a clown has become a highly visible signifier within the context of the 'suburban uncanny' and the field of horror studies in general. While far from the first film to use the physicality and the presence of clowns to represent cultural fears or to present a distorted or painted human image hidden behind make-up or disguise to incite horror—something that Tobe Hooper himself had already done to great effect in his prior film *The Funhouse* (1981)—*Poltergeist*'s use of Robbie's toy clown has become a well-known agent of 'kindertrauma'.

Figure 3.2. The clown

Initially the clown in *Poltergeist* is presented as a passive (if disturbing) toy clown, a standout and slightly out of place artefact among the memorabilia, toys, dolls, and knick-knacks that adorn the two younger Freelings's shared room. The clown is initially presented to be a somewhat shapeless thing, with a flamboyant ruffled costume concealing its body but with distorted and elongated appendages and a slightly dead-eyed painted fully whitened mask onto a plastic moulded head. While

POLTERGEIST

the clown is unsettling and unnerving it is a passive object, and while not overtly sinister in appearance it is an object that is evidenced to personally disturb Robbie. The underpinning and foreshadowing of the clown's eventual malevolency are evident in Robbie's reaction towards it, as it is coded to be an object that fits both within the realm of the realistic and also the uncanny. It is both a physical manifestation and personalised apparition of a childhood phobia that incites intrinsic fear within Robbie and an object that personally haunts him throughout the film. Robbie's personal mechanism to deal with this objectified fear is shown to be via a good aim and a readily available Chewbacca jacket. It is implied that this action has been performed many times before and that covering the clown alleviates the fear of it staring at him in bed.

While the initial presentation of the clown toy is shown to induce fear this fear is presented initially as unjustified. While not pleasant the clown is an inanimate object, much smaller than Robbie and holds no real physical threat. The fear of the object is purely psychological on Robbie's part and, as Hofmann (2008) describes, is a 'cognitive process of fear acquisition applied to the object'. As such, when the poltergeists imbue the clown with spiritual energy the malevolence of the clown is doubled, as it now presents both an object that invokes fear and now is also one that is a physical threat.

The clown's potential capability to do physical harm while foreshadowed in the film is more evident in the novelisation of the film. The clown in the novel moves around the house by itself, appearing in various rooms where it was not put down. The clown also appears outside in a scene not presented in the film that describes Robbie's birthday party. The other more startling incident in the novel shows that something bites Robbie and while the family put it down to vermin in the house it is evident that it is the clown that has caused this (again supporting the notion of the child-like behaviour of biting shown by the spirits in the narrative). Within the film the implication is that the clown will eventually come to life (Mackley, 2016) and the anticipation of this is repeatedly teased. When this actually occurs, it provides one of the most chilling scenes of the text, set up by having Robbie waking up, looking at the chair, and noting that the clown is not present. This initial terror is enhanced by invoking other childhood fears (the fear of monsters under the bed) as he searches for the clown under his own bed, again not finding it. While the clown itself is a frightening apparition, the absence of the clown on the chair and indeed under the bed enhances the fear in this scene with viewers pre-

45

DEVIL'S ADVOCATES

empting that the clown may have come to life but not knowing where it is. Not having it under the bed and drawing out and extending this terror by its absence is masterfully done, so much so that when the clown does finally appear behind Robbie as he sits up the audience is already overwrought and on edge so that the tension on this jump scare is amplified considerably. Adding an additional layer of menace, the clown is not represented as it has been throughout the film; it has gone through a metamorphosis with the slightly dead eyed but essentially friendly face gone to be replaced by a warped, distorted representation. It is now an angry, possessed, demonic entity that ferociously drags Robbie under the bed, which supposedly on-set caused actor Oliver Robbins to be choked in real life.

The representation of the clown as a trickster and having the agency to induce fear within the text underpins the revulsion initially triggered by the Uncanny Valley phenomenon of the malevolent portrayal of the toy clown within the film going against the tradition of the clown as a whimsical character. The image of the '*Poltergeist* clown' still resonates within the context of horror iconography, providing a potent vehicle for the suburban uncanny. The unpredictability and otherness of the representations of clowns in other texts also underpins the important component of 'creepiness' of the clown within *Poltergeist* (Castelli, 2017) with the final manifestation of the possessed clown adding to reviews, critiques, and commentary that perpetuate the notion of the potential connection between clowns and the supernatural, or that a clown is in some way a type of supernatural entity (Durwin, 2004).

3.5 THERE'S NO PLACE LIKE HOME: THE IMPORTANCE OF *THE WIZARD OF OZ*

Writing in *The Baum Bugle*, Elms (1983) states that numerous fantasy and science-fiction films derive their themes and imagery from MGM's *The Wizard of Oz* (1939), and Spielberg's *Close Encounters*, *E.T.*, and indeed *Poltergeist* itself can be seen to share motifs, themes and iconography evident in that film. Spielberg's fascination with fairy tales, classical children's novels, and 'old Hollywood' is prevalent within his films, with both *E.T.*'s and *Poltergeist*'s representations of their environment sharing similarities with Frank L. Baum's portrayal of Oz as 'a genteel critique of commodity fetishism' (Culver, 1998).

The representation of Cuesta Verde within *Poltergeist* is a literal modern take on the Emerald City, described as Baum's 'Consumer Paradise' set not in Oz but rather within the affluent emerald-green rolling hills of 1980s California.

This 'Oz-ification' (Chaston, 1997) of the environment within *Poltergeist* allows for the transition between the context of normality within the film's digenesis into that of the realms of fantasy, allowing for logical step-changes in the transition of narrative from melodrama into the 'Suburban Fantastic' (McFadzean, 2017). Apart from the obvious part that Tangina plays within the text as both a fairy godmother/good Witch and Munchkin the text provides two initial natural metaphors for this change, the first one being the initial storm that gathers over Cuesta Verde, the other being an earthquake, both natural occurrences that are not uncommon within California.

While thunder and lightning can be explained, defined, and quantified, which Steven tries to do for Robbie within the text, spending time with him to contextualise the natural aspects of the storm within the definitions of time and distance (which makes little difference as both he and Carol Anne end up in their parents' bed), the representation of a storm within the text is anything but natural, instead being a signifier of unnatural disruption to the perceived order of family life. The storm represented as a thing of malevolence rather than a natural occurrence can also be seen within *The Wizard of Oz* where Dorothy sees the chaos of the storm within the vortex as well as Miss Gulch's transformation into the Wicked Witch of the West—a stark visual representation of the transition from her environment from one of normality to one of the more fantastical.

The storm within *Poltergeist* mirrors the storm in *The Wizard of Oz* as being the catalyst to trigger the transformation of the narrative into the 'uncanny'—a storm is often a symbol or signifier for upheaval or coded as a catalyst for change. As the ghosts 'punch' their way into the house causing an earthquake within the bedroom (again something that can be explained as a natural phenomenon) as well as the 'spectral light' represented as iridescent electro-static blue bursting through the wall into the house that could be construed as a short or electrical fault caused by the storm again plausible within the remit of new houses being built and natural phenomenon.

These signifiers all represent a narrative shift allowing the text to go *'Over the rainbow'* into the realms of the fantastical. The family and environment have not geographically moved and, unlike Dorothy, are not physically ripped up by a tornado and transposed somewhere else (this of course happens later) but the stages of Joseph Campbell's Hero's Journey are enabled to take place.

The ever-present storm is repeatedly shown within the film as a dark (yet colourful) brooding mass over the estate and specifically over the house in stark visual contrast to the otherwise blue summer skies shown throughout the film. Rather than the on-set storms and hidden effects of waddling boards or flashing stoplights that represent rolling thunder and lightning that would envelope traditional gothic horror environments of the past the optical effects that represent the storm in *Poltergeist* undulate in an almost organic natural way and are a testimony to the visual effects team who by using oils and paints in back-lit water tanks matted onto the film present a dark shifting menace that is a signifier of the malevolence to come.

Figure 3.3. Storm

The environmental change that the storm brings allows for the fantastical and terrifying to usurp realism within the text, while the foreshadowing of the 'wise old tree' in the garden is initially described as benevolent once again by Steven to appease Robbie and to counteract his childhood fear of seeing faces in the trunk. As he explains: 'It was here for a long time. Long before my company built this neighbourhood...it knows everything about us.'

Robbie is justified in his fear as the tree does indeed 'know everything' about the family,

POLTERGEIST

making his nightmare become a reality in his staged abduction, being the first object within the narrative to become possessed, turning against the family, and personally attacking him, but as is shown the intelligence of the protagonists is the parallel abduction of Carol Anne with the tree not actually wanting to consume him at all.

Represented as a mass of branches distorted into makeshift arms, hands, and fingers the tree proves to be similar in appearance to the possessed forest within *The Evil Dead* (1981) but even more so to the humanised and aggressive 'Fighting Trees' shown within *The Wizard of Oz*, which use their branches to throw apples at Dorothy. While not humanised in such a way by presenting a face or voice the tree is shown, however, to have a vast, cavernous mouth by which it attempts to eat him, while at the same time the same malevolent force abducts Carol Anne.

While the tree scene could have been seen as comedic without context with the practical effects representing a monstrous sentient tree full off probing branch fingers looking to abduct and eat a child, the direction and framing of the scene within the midst of the storm, which has Robbie battered, bloodied, and bruised, is presented as harrowing and brutal. Once again, a scenario is transplanted from the fairy-tale forest of northern Europe to a suburban back-garden and that's what really scares—the notion that the dark, unexplained mediaeval supernatural elements has laid dormant until this modern age of reason and technology and we still cannot overcome them.

The definition and context of the underlying horror is what is highly prevalent within the text. Logic and reasoning dictate that the tapping of the branches on the window during a storm are a natural phenomenon caused by wind, glass, and wood; however, mapping these sounds into the context of a child's imagination and the definitions of what is real, logical, and natural are soon replaced with primeval childhood trauma and fear. The tree is tapping to get your attention, making you aware that it can see you and it intends to eat you. This additional element of imagination supersedes logic and presents a scenario that is terrifying beyond all reason. Even the reassurance of authority and being assisted by your parents does not help and as the narrative of *Poltergeist* shows that even those with maturing and agency for reassurance are of no assistance, as the sly and crafty things from the other side are more intelligent, distracting everyone and doing something more terrifying by taking away a loved one.

DEVIL'S ADVOCATES

Within this scene the storm imagery is highlighted as the battle to save Robbie moves outside where a stylised tornado is shown in a similar manner as *The Wizard of Oz*. While the family fight to save their son from the tree the poltergeists achieve their objective with Carol Anne and once this occurs stop the charade with the tree, which is then sucked up by the tornado (again in the same manner as *The Evil Dead*), a discarded plaything used in the deception but worthless now that the spirits have Carol Anne, and within the narrative the transition into the realms of the fantastical and the overturning of normality is now complete.

Figure 3.4. Sinister tree

3.6 ENTER 'THE BEAST'

While establishing the setting of *Poltergeist* Spielberg intentionally removes 'gothic' trappings and traditions of mountains, monasteries, and sweeping stately homes, replacing with acres of housing, Californian sunshine, and the ideal family environment where safety and nurturing are still paramount. The traditional horror film has supplied the nature needed to produce the right kind of monster 'for the times' with the spirits in *Poltergeist* being this—a modern interpretation of age-old spirits but using modern technology with a modern setting to do something that had been represented in films for decades.

While other haunted house movies from the late 1970s and early 1980s have similar insidious evil entities as the antagonist with *Burnt Offerings* (1976), *The Amityville Horror*

POLTERGEIST

and *The Shining* (1980) presenting hidden malevolent spirts or supernatural entities intent to do harm. The main antagonists of *Poltergeist*, however, are initially represented as playful children but as the narrative unfolds the layers of danger and the menace increases with the use of trickery and guile evident in the spirits' abduction of Carol Anne who covert her and her light.

The reveal of the figurative and literal underlying menace within the narrative of the restless souls trapped in the burial ground below the house provide a solid foundation on which Spielberg builds the mythology and narrative around the concept of poltergeists. The antagonists in *Poltergeist* are something unique—they are never named, catalogued, nor explained, and the lights, the movement, and the context of them are ill-defined and vague. Within the progression of the film, however, Tangina reveals that the other side/afterlife has a form of hierarchy and that the initial unnamed spirits as well as Carol Anne are being trapped by something else—a monstrous, more sinister malevolent entity than the poltergeists themselves described as 'The Beast'.

The Beast is a ruler of pseudo-hell and while there are no visualisations of the traditional depiction of hells (fire brimstone, torture, and lost souls) with the 'Other Side', which is eventually seen in the second film, it is visualised as an ethereal space, a dead, empty environment tinged the unnatural light. In the first film, however, the realm of the 'Other Side' is presented as backlit high-intensity spotlights from which things emerge from the light, not the darkness reminiscent of the representation and colour scheme used to bring forth the Cenobites in *Hellraiser* (1987). As such, the 'Other Side' is not underground or under the house the Freelings live in but rather an ethereal plane of existence in which their house is a portal to access.

The Beast, while not represented as a traditional demon, reinterpretation of the devil or Satan in the sense of the context of the Christian beliefs still has agency and 'commands' the other spirits within this realm. It is described as hiding Carol Anne from the other spirits and keeping her for his own. By not giving The Beast of the other antagonists of the film names it codes it (or them) as a 'thing'. By attributing a depersonalising noun creates the implications of the nature of the antagonist rather than what or who it is, describing something as a beast provides the connotations of something objectionable or unpleasant, something that is cruel, violent, and not human.

51

DEVIL'S ADVOCATES

Within the text viewers are also presented with various forms of the physical manifestation of The Beast. In one of the key (and visually stunning) set-pieces of the film the text provides viewers with a physical manifestation of the trapped poltergeists as they glide down the staircase in the impressive optical light-show and, while disturbing, these scenes are passive, intent on showing the 'trapped' nature of the spirits on the other side. They are ethereally beautiful, frightening due to their 'Otherness', but also graceful and elegant and do not interact or register that the family and surroundings are there—they are trapped in their own realm and have no agency or awareness of the family and that they are being monitored or scrutinised.

Within the original screenplay and the novelisation of the film by James Kahn (1982) there is a scene where the true nature of The Beast is revealed. This first manifestation of The Beast appears in Ryan's video footages where he is presented as a menacing controlling figure, a cruel old man who is later revealed in the film's sequels to be Reverend Henry Kane. The Beast in human form guides the other ghosts through the house. These spirts again in the screenplay and novel are named and have larger roles in the narrative. The film provided glimpses of these spirits such as the Lady in Waiting who later in the novel aids the family on the 'Other Side'. As with their visualisation on screen the spirits are described as passive, white, glowing, and ethereal whereas The Beast is described as a malevolent, dark presence fully aware and even acknowledging the family and scientist who are observing him. Again in the screenplay and novel The Beast within this scene stares back at them and even smiles, providing a little more context to the shot where Diane exclaims, 'That thing is in there with my baby.' A final significant variation seen in the novelisation compared to the film is that The Beast is named. In the novel Tangina identifies the entity, naming it as 'Ghala' (from the Arabic translation of the word 'ghoul'), stating that it is, 'A paltry name, not even so base. It surprises me not, that you would not say it. It must be an embarrassment to you. Ghala.'

The first 'official' on-screen appearance of The Beast, however, comes towards the end of the film during the climax of the rescue of Carol Anne. Within this set-piece the family, headed by Diane and directed by Tangina, have already engaged with and entered the 'Other Side', using the rope to navigate and retrieve Carol Anne. During Tangina's contradictory directions and statement and that 'all are welcome in the light' a miscommunication occurs between Tangina and Steven and, for a split second, he does

POLTERGEIST

not do what he is told. In this confusion the family left behind in Carol Anne's bedroom are confronted by a vast demonic face that appears out of the closet/portal as The Beast attempts to block the rescue of both Carol Anne and now Diane who are both now in the other side.

Craig Readon in an interview with *Rue Morgue Magazine* (2012) notes that the visual effects for The Beast for this scene were intended to be significantly different with the apparition of The Beast, which is seen on film with the initial design of this monstrous face, initially intended to be more human and akin to the 'look' of Lon Chaney Jr compared to the vast decaying bestial apparition that was used.

A secondary appearance of The Beast, which is in-keeping with the animalistic interpretation of the film's antagonist, is during the film's 'second ending', as the poltergeists in a final effort attempt to re-abduct Carol Anne and to stop the family, especially Diane, from reaching them. The 'Door Guardian' is a massive, white, predatory, and bird-like (potentially mirroring Carol Anne's dead bird Tweety) manifestation that has her recall and scream in fright. The apparition is presented as a huge, dominating, and vicious paranormal attack-dog/sentry intent from stooping access to where the children are being abducted. While physically imposing the addition of the extraordinary and abhorrent are present as the creature is yet still skeletal and translucent in appearance covered in wispy, thin, stringy, fibres and white hair and potentially the same unseen entity that attacked Marty previously.

In each manifestation, The Beast resembles something unnatural and impure presentenced in the context of the monstrous and inhuman, a rotting form of something dead, decaying, and decomposing representing that which is buried in the ground below the Freelings's house, the human bodies in the cemetery, and later Carol Anne's deceased bird. The evil force of The Beast can be read as the past coming back for vengeance or unnatural 'other'—a primal terror designed and presented as something that knows what the family will be fearful of to stop them from rescuing their daughter.

While the manifestation of The Beast is bestial in the first film it is worth noting that the entity tries a differing approach to regaining Carol Anne in the sequels. The large monstrous physical representations are replaced, using the tactics of guile and

DEVIL'S ADVOCATES

persuasion, humanising the inhuman in the form of Reverend Henry Kane in the sequel. Portrayed by actor Julian Beck Kane is presented as a dark, bastardised, holy man, a paternal figure attempting to take over the responsibilities from Steven for the caring and nurturing of his family. While Steven is not an absent father there is the notion of an external force forcibly interjecting into a family with the insistence and intent that they can do a better job of leading the family, leading to one of the most intense and iconic battles of wills within cinematic horror, with the rain, skeletal nature of the gravely ill Beck, and the false rictus grin all adding to the menace of The Beast wanting to be let in.

While this personification and humanisation of The Beast in the sequel takes away from the abstract notion of invisible supernaturally powerful spirits in the first film the framing of the protagonist/antagonist is now presented in the context of 'equals'—Kane is perceived by the audience as a person and as such the threat and framing of his malevolence must differ from the first film.

Visually, Kane is an amalgamation of historical Americanised horror—a Jonestown style preacher (Miller, 2013) of the 'American Gothic' style and a supernatural embodiment of the pitchfork-holding man from the American Gothic painting by Grant Wood (painted as an approximation of his dentist Dr Byron McKeeby). The signifiers of the wide-brimmed hat and skeletal frame/sunken eyes are also part of stylised cowboy/Wild-Western representation of death or the Grim Reaper—a living embodiment of the pale rider based on classical painting or indeed the description of Charon the ferryman from Greek mythology. His personality, mannerisms, and demeanour are presented in a similar fashion to another iconic cinematic Western preacher, 'reverend' Harry Powell— the antagonist from *The Night of the Hunter* (1955). While Robert Mitchum's preacher/ serial killer 'is one of the most frightening of movies, with one of the most unforgettable of villains' (Ebert, 1996). Kane takes all this character's 'charm' and twists his power of determination, conviction in his 'lord', and beguiling false charisma for the ulterior motives to the point of addiction and near obsession of reclaiming Carol Anne.

'The Beast' as the main antagonist of the *Poltergeist* series, whether as a monstrous spirit or personified 'avatar' inhabiting Reverend Kane, is framed as the culmination and manifestation of the anger, hatred, and eventual malevolence of the spirts trapped under the house, creating an identifiable and quantifiable supernatural antagonist for the

54

films. Framing the main antagonist as an identifiable 'Beast' rather than a collection of unspecified or unnamed entities quantifies the film's antagonists, allowing the audience to connect with the film—a Beast is something that can be faced and defeated within a traditional cinematic narrative. While the unidentified spirits in *Poltergeist* have had their graves sullied and a lack of respect shown for their passing these transgressive actions needed to be framed into a traditional plot device of one antagonist for the family to overcome, banish, or defeat, and makes for a far more emotive and engaging final act compared to the family confronting the more faceless or invisible antagonists such as the initial poltergeists or the unseen real estate company whom both Steven and Teague work for who really are the main villains of the film.

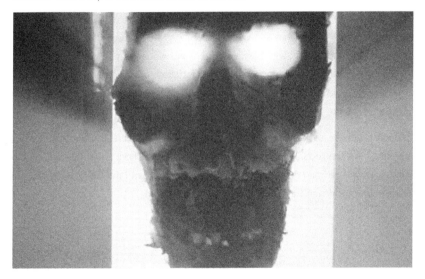

Figure 3.5. The Beast

Debating that the real villain of the piece to indeed be the real estate company could be seen that the drive for all the film's antagonists is similar in needs and motivation in the need to covert something; for the spirits and Beast it is the drive for Carol Anne and her pureness and for the corporations behind the housing estate it's the drive for profit and financial gain.

It also alludes to the continued themes from *The Wizard of Oz* present in the film in that the main antagonist is not an all-powerful supernatural entity, but rather actually a human being hidden behind a literal curtain, happy pulling the strings from a distance. With a veritable smoke and mirror show provided by the poltergeists, the actual manifestation and horror they present to the Freelings could be deemed to be a by-product and distraction for the greater evils of the consumer greed mentality, an invisible enemy driving this and that remains even after the Freelings escape and the house implodes into itself.

By creating this other 'conceptual bogeyman' of corporate greed manifesting whose actions of corner and cost cutting coupled with the lack of empathy makes the housing estate company more inhuman than the inhuman presence of the spirits invading the house. The lack of humanity shown by corporations are far more horrific than apparitions and ghostly encounters with Spielberg and Hooper emphasising the point that the real 'modern monsters' are societal manifestations of greed, profits, and the need to need driven by an unseen malevolent force but one very much based in 1980s corporate America.

The victim of these actions therefore could be seen to be both the Freeling family themselves and the souls trapped under the house, both of whom are at the whim of forces far greater than themselves and by whose actions both the family and those buried below are driven into a purgatory not of their making.

CHAPTER 4: THE AMERICAN DREAM/THE AMERICAN NIGHTMARE—THE POLITICS OF *POLTERGEIST*

During the New Hollywood Cinema movement of the 1960s and 1970s the portrayal of the 'nuclear family stereotype' and their associated lifestyles often portrayed in mainstream Hollywood cinema in the 1950s slowly receded, allowing for texts to showcase films that tackled growing diversification, social realism, and the changing attitudes and outlooks, providing a better representation of the real cultural shifts that were affecting American society during these decades.

The growth of second-wave feminism, for example, provided a catalyst for the visual portrayal of the empowerment of women on-screen in mainstream films such as *Bonnie and Clyde* (1967) or *The Graduate* (1967) as well as presenting female characters in roles of authority or agents of change. The growth of cinematic sub-genres and exploitation texts (be that 'Grindhouse', 'Blaxploitation', or 'Martial Arts' films) provided a plethora of cinematic representation. Shifting political opinion and purposeful representation of the 'Other' within sub-genres such as horror provided critique on social and political issues such as the growing anti-war sentiment of these decades as well as presenting a far more 'realistic' portrayal of modern America. *Poltergeist*, coming at the end of New Hollywood's reign, moved horror back for the spotlight of the plight of the middle classes and the move to the suburban that were portrayed during the 1950s, a whole generation before Hollywood's new wave inception.

This return to lost American values of 'conservativism' and into a more understandable and relatable setting of suburban comfort is a key discursive point of *Poltergeist*—it is a text that represents the rebellion of the 1960s, growing up and conforming to the very elements that they themselves rebelled against. This move back to the idealised 'American Dream' concept, however, is purposely tainted as Hooper and Spielberg introduce the horror of the 'Other' into the safe spaces of middle-America. This unwanted presence into the idealised conservative middle-class setting had invaded and was now presented on the artificial streets, behind the manicured shrubberies or preaching door to door.

DEVIL'S ADVOCATES

4.1 THE IMPORTANCE OF THE BABY BOOMERS

Within the film both Steven and Diane are coded as affluent parents being part of the social demographic designated as 'Baby Boomers' (or Boomers)—the catchment of people born from the 1940s to the 1960s, and the first American 'post-war' generation. These individuals were nurtured and grew up in a time that saw an increase in affluence and an increased standard of living for all due to widespread government reforms, which included subsidies in essentials such as housing and education. Within the narrative viewers are presented with the results of this generation gains in these areas 'spoilt' with these opportunities and being able to flourish with the Freelings typifying the 'grown-up' boomer generation benefiting greatly from these conditions.

Representation of the Freelings as 'Boomers' defines them to a generation provided with opportunity but also one that also looked for aspiration and improvement against a social backdrop that allowed them to do so. This opportunity was provided by the wider political framing provided to them by Ronald Reagan and conservative agenda during the late 1970s. Being the Governor of California from 1967 to 1975 it was Reagan who presided over the 'Cuesta Verde-isation' of the region (with his own ranch just down the road from Simi Valley). This new opportunity is established within the opening shots of *Poltergeist* as we are shown briefly sets of advertising signs/billboards for 'Cuesta Verde Sales Information & Model Homes', establishing the context of the aspiration of homeownership gained through hard work, endeavour, and drive in the construction of both literal and figurative idealised 'All-American' home life.

This presentation of Reagan's 1980s American Dream being lived by and embraced wholeheartedly by the Boomers generation is presented in numerous ways on screen from the initial gathering of the Freelings's friends, who are representations of themselves (middle-class, early to middle aged, conservative males), socially together in their spacious house, invited over to 'watch the game' (American Football) while consuming junk snacks, food, and beers—a very middle-class activity and is in many ways as surface, synthetic, and superficial as the houses they live in.

The film's representation of this vast affluent suburb that homed the growing middle classes represents the growth of conservativism and the return to 'traditional' values of home and self-improvement that has become the atypical representation of 1980s political thinking especially those of Ronald Reagan's presidency whose laissez-faire attitude of 'free economics' and the weakening of regulation presented a supposed environment of enterprise, expansion, and profit. While the film was released in in 1982 on the cusp of Reagan winning the election in 1980 the ideas of de-regulation to increase productivity, generate wealth, and of course profit represents one of the key plot points of the text, that of the drive of the real-estate companies to chase the highest profits possible by doing the quickest and easiest job possible in the build of the houses of the Cuesta Verde estate.

With the initial long-distance set-ups of the film establishing the vast entirety of the Cuesta Verde valleys' suburban sprawl the camera focuses on the streets of the estate, following Steven's friend on his makeshift delivery service through the identikit houses and overly manicured front lawns of the estate, eventually pin-pointing and focusing upon the Freelings's house, purposely designed to be unidentifiable among the many similar looking properties. Within the trailer and initial few minutes of the film itself the emphasis is purposely and obviously to present a *'generically modelled'* environment as Neale (1999) asserts that 'horror conventions condition both production and reception and thus instantly propel the spectator into a—by then—carefully formatted atmosphere'.

The ideals of Boomers benefiting from the growing ethos of *Reaganomics* is presented in an obvious manner with Steven being shown to be reading the president's book in bed. While this is an obvious indication of the views and outlook, politics, and worldview that the Freelings (especially Steven) have and aspire towards there is an implication in his attire (the reading glasses) that he is trying to become more 'mature' and to understand and be part of this 'new' way of political thinking. It is heavily implied that both Steven and Diane were initially a lot more liberal in their thinking, being a very carefree and free-spirited couple in younger life as the political reading, glasses, and attitude is juxtaposed with the couple smoking a joint, an obvious signifier that the growing conservativism ethos and outlook has not quite taken hold completely.

The more liberal attitude of the couple's earlier life is implied to have had to change due to their personal circumstances as suggested in that text that Diane became pregnant at an early age and as such there was a need and requirement to 'grow up'

DEVIL'S ADVOCATES

and take responsibility for the forthcoming arrival of their first child Dana. *Poltergeist*, in its contradictory facets, provides contradiction in this representation of the Freelings. Steven Freeling is noted to be 40 while Diane is 32. However, their daughter Dana (who as a character is underrepresented in the text) is 16, from which we can infer that Diane gave birth when she was 16 and Steven was 24 (a highly problematic social scenario, even in the 1980s). This family dynamic is explored in a little more detail via the novelisation of the film, which states that Diane is Steven's second wife and Dana is her stepdaughter; however, in the film there is no reference made to this as such, creating a family dynamic that is questionable. During this period (16 years) since the Freelings's first child was born, the shift from this carefree and more spiritual outlook is clear and superseded by the requirement for responsibility and perceived maturity milestones that come with it, embedded within the context of the 'American Dream'. As such, the free-thinking almost hippy-like carefree lifestyle by necessity is replaced by the drive to find and secure well-paid steady work with the intent to buy a 'dream home' and in turn fill the house full of material goods. The inherent emotional and instilled paternal nature to provide and nurture are superseded very quickly by these social factors and a loving, satisfied, content, and 'happy' family environment are lost along the way. This drive for improvement means that some of the core elements that *Poltergeist*'s narrative is based upon (love and security and a strong family bond) initially come far below the hierarchy of importance within the initial setting and narrative of the text with factors such as the need for continual drive for improvement of the home environment, work pressures, and the use of the television to entertain and 'nanny' the children all assisting in diluting the need to nurture and in turn creating a fractured family dynamic—issues of course that are queried, debated, and resolved within the film's themes.

These dimensions of surface and the synthetic presentations of the Freelings's environment, lifestyle choice, and career that drive them towards the standardised ideals of the 'American Dream' are not inherently evil; these are archetypal family problems and environments and are not used to define, objectify, or pass judgement on the Freelings's lifestyle choices but are there to reinforce the normalcy of the family. These definitions are human nature. The Freelings are of course defined by social, political, and personal drives and choices—this is one of the successes of the text: the Freelings are portrayed as rounded, three-dimensional characters. They are not action heroes, they are not extraordinary, and they do not have any atypical features that make them different from anyone else—they are for all intents and purposes perfectly normal people living perfectly normal lives. This perceived normality and lack of anything 'special' is also reinforced to an even greater extent in the scene in which Steven is shown selling a house to another generic family. The couple not only look and act like them but he is showing them exactly the same house that his family lives in but by a clever transition from the Freelings's house full of goods to exactly the same space of another identical house but without the accreuments of a busy family—he is selling therefore not only the space of the house itself but also the goals and lifestyle choices that this couple are intending to aspire towards—essentially the same middle-class 'vanilla' ordinariness of the Freelings themselves. In representing and in fine tuning the bland and generic nature of the family, surroundings, and environment Spielberg and Hooper extenuate the abnormal events that happen within the narrative of the text and the success of *Poltergeist* as a film resting on these themes.

Figure 4.1. The Freelings's lifestyle

4.2 'GREED IS GOOD' (WALL STREET, 1987)

According to Michelson (2018), the mid-twentieth-century consumer represented by the Freeling family is not driven by genuine need, but by a 'need to need'. It is this insatiable 'need to need' that feeds the notion of commercialism that is so relevant in 1980s cultural representation. It is this consumerism and drive to want that underpin

DEVIL'S ADVOCATES

soul-destroying qualities of the perfect suburbia in which they live—an innate focus on striving for a perfect lifestyle that will never quite be perfect enough. It is with throwaway lines of the text such as Carol Anne's innocent line of, 'Oh well...Can I get a goldfish?' that Hooper and Spielberg can highlight the lack of appreciation for the material—products, consumables, and even life itself are replaceable and hold no value to a generation brought up by the comforts of material wealth that middle-class suburbia provide. While released at the beginning of the decade *Poltergeist* can as such be read as a forerunner to Oliver Stone's indictment of capitalism. The implication of 'Greed is good' made famous in *Wall Street* (1987) can be seen to bookend the notion of the Reagan administration where wealth was intended to generate no matter what the wider implications or cost.

The context and dialogue throughout *Poltergeist* indicate that the Freelings have been working through their adult life to achieve a certain lifestyle (be that through necessity of family circumstances or actual personal drive) and to continually strive towards the aspects of the 'American Dream' fulfilment. The opening sequence and indeed the beginning of the film is full of images that symbolise these aspirational qualities and these signifiers for drive to aspire towards something more, a large house in a cul-de-sac in a happy suburbia full of consumer goods and pop culture memorabilia. Ronald Reagan, and his 'Morning in America' slogan, show up again and again, instilling the messages of conservatism and free market economics.

The environment in which the Freeling children are bought up is represented within *Poltergeist* as a buy/consume/dispose mentality imprinted on them by their parents and cultural stereotypes, surroundings, and political environment, which by the 1980s came to represent the very epitome of consumerism and a set of values that relegated all other forms of 'value' as a secondary concern. The 1980s saw the drive to provide an appeasement of appetites in any form possible, be it through household goods, food, or entertainment spectacles such as films, sporting events, or multi-channel television—all presented within the text within the first few minutes.

This perceived perfect 1980s family unit is also defined by Cohen (2003) and must adhere to strict gender roles, promoted as the best and most 'American' kind of family—something to which the average American could and should be aspiring towards. Once the family unit is established, they could then buy homes and consume goods, keeping the larger economy buoyant. As a result, Americans and suburbanites within 1980s texts are in a manner portrayed as a swath of consumers rather than individuals, driven by consumerism, with the parents presented in a hetero-monogamous relationship and the family presented as one of atypical conservative values with an implied need for social conformity—all of which resonated with the audiences of the 'Reagan-era' political environment.

Deeper and more mindful aspects of modern life have been relegated through the drive and promise of expansion, for bigger housing developments, bigger televisions, bigger pools, bigger bank balances. It is this removal of the aspects of contentment, the importance of family over goods, and 'love' over need that underpin the text and could be debated to be a spiritual problem, not so much the context of the belief of a 'god' but rather the *disrespect* for life, the natural world, and the notion of the spirit and the afterlife.

While the notion of the 1980s capitalist mantra of 'Greed is good' established in Oliver Stone's *Wall Street* (1987) had not really started in earnest in film when *Poltergeist* was released in the early 1980s the corporatised 'evils' of short cutting on jobs and producing content 'on-the-cheap' in the pursuit of profit is evident throughout the film—from the houses being built too close as to effect the remote control 'signals' of the television to the lights of the Freeling house fusing to nightmare-inducing scenes of the bodies left in the cemetery by the company that emerge towards the finale of the film in the swimming pool. The company Steven sells for short-changing consumers and the residents of the estate on shabbily build, bad quality environments is as much an antagonist as the poltergeists themselves—a horror of a faceless company driven by the obsession with profitability, trapping individuals into this system of greed within the estate, the home, and even beyond the grave itself.

4.3 THE REPRESENTATION OF THE NUCLEAR FAMILY

Jeanne Halls' commentary on film (2000) is that narratives are best understood in relation to the 'periods in which they were produced and consumed'. By acknowledging this statement in regard to the representation of the Freeling family structure and environment they are typified depictions of an early 1980s 'nuclear family'. The Freelings, while not high in social status, are defined to be moderately wealthy middle-class earners, with Steven Freeling (as a typified 'bread-winner') recognised as good at his job. The Freelings's social mobility, education, and prospects as well as the obvious accruements that this lifestyle would typically bring are all present in the text—they live in a large modern house, have multiple televisions and gaming consoles, merchandised children's bedsheets, and an abundance of branded goods, toys, and costly foodstuff (steak in the fridge, for example). This is middle-class affluence defined and represented on a scale of the 'perceived income' from Steven's well-paid job and, as such, creates believable atmosphere and surroundings to have us as an audience acknowledge this realistic environment and that he can sustain and support three children in highly comfortable surroundings.

The building of the swimming pool also shows social standing and drive for more opulent surroundings; the Freelings can not only afford a swimming pool but can also sub-contract and outsource the work to a more working-class demographic. This delegation of manual work goes with an emerging suburban-yuppie in Steven and social family depiction would be atypical of a 'white collar' working male delegating to 'blue collar' working males. There is no hyper-realisation in the depiction of the family identifiers and signifiers—that is the social standing of the atypical affluent middle-class American family of the time.

Both parents seem to be educated to a high level and are articulate and 'well-bred' and there are suggestions and implications that Diane has come from a social bracket of a 'higher' upper middle class. Within the second film we see this to be true as we gain access to a point of Diane's family (mother) and her pre-married environment—she herself has grown up in a similar loving, moneyed, middle-class family home to that portrayed by the Freeling household.

Wood (1986) suggests that the typical American family, as represented by the Freelings, is presented as a 'cellular construction, institutionalised by capitalism and patriarchal relations and values'. Other comparative texts of the time suggest the pre-structured conventions of the conservative nuclear family stereotype are more disjointed, fragmented, and more reflective of their audience rather than the stylised pre-conception: families split by divorce or 'latchkey kids' with both parents working (to sustain the level of income and lifestyle required for the settings of these films) all present in films of this era—Michael, Elliott, and Gertie within *E.T.*, for example, are all brought up by a single mother.

Kellner (1983c) notes that since the 1970s horror scholarship had already highlighted the genre's historical engagement with shifting political, economic, and social anxieties representing excesses 'at home' (as within the context of American society) within the digenesis of horror taking place within a family home scenario, presenting them as environments of aggression and repression in texts such as *Carrie* (1976), *The Shining*, and *The Amityville Horror*, examples of transgressive family environments representing the socio-economic shifts of American social values and makeup at that time. Hooper had already dealt with familial issues in *The Texas Chain Saw Massacre*, in which the cannibal family is, up to a point, sympathetic—their bonds and tensions were familiar elements that we cannot truly disassociate ourselves from, with no matter how monstrous their behaviour. *The Texas Chain Saw Massacre* is a solid example of a director commenting through film narratives on the excesses of society, using the framework of a toxic family environment. The gore and viscera might well be implied and not seen but it is the harrowing family environment and the excess of the patriarchy (Mehls, 2015) that is represented as the real horror on display.

4.4 ORGANISED CHAOS

Dee Hock's management theory of 'chaordic organisations' seems quite apt to define the representation of family within *Poltergeist*. His suggestion of 'chaordic organisations'—a scenario consisting of one of chaos and order to create a harmonious existence, which exists due to a 'difficult and painful process filled with joy and humour' (Hock, 1999)—epitomises the Freelings. Muir (2002) also comments on the text's organised chaos, choosing to compare the families' multiple threads of conversation and action over breakfast to that of the example within *E.T.* where Elliot's 'extended' family are playing *Dungeons & Dragons*.

Chaordic theory within families shows that even within the interpersonal there is still some form of recognisable hierarchy and structure and the Freelings, while dysfunctional, are essentially a 'good' family. The horror that besets them is external in nature overlaid onto the family rather than coming from within and from an internal source, defined and coded as an attack on family values, the fear of losing control and losing the established way of living via this intrusion of the home and family environment by the 'Other'.

Whereas *E.T.* accepts 'Otherness' into the patriarchal family unit and in so doing there is some benevolence, in *Poltergeist* there is an earlier acceptance (especially by Diane) of the Other and of the unusual within the same family hierarchical structure. A premature acceptance that is repeated later, when external forces are requested for assistance, but there is the turn back to introversion and the importance of the family unit and the same wide-eyed optimism as *E.T.*, although this acceptance instead of being mutual becomes one-sided and malevolent.

This threat of the 'Other' in the texts is initially represented by the intrusion of a differing economic class, with the blue-collar construction workers intruding within the middle-class bourgeois spaces, taking liberties with established boundaries, initially with inappropriate overtly sexualised comments towards Dana followed in the same scene by an intrusion by 'Bluto' helping himself to food through the window. This invasive move into defined pre-established bourgeois space overlays deeper routed insecurities of the middle class of the time, those of potential economic depression or the loss of control of family or offspring. These fears are repeated often in similar 1980s narratives highlighting the middle class's attempts to stem either social change or perceived delinquency of youth with the growth of institutions and programmes to assist parents with these issues.

The film in showing Carol Anne separated from her family presents an image of the disintegration of the family unit. The family unit's degradation is also shown as older sister Dana not being present for significant parts of the film either away 'at friends' or either doing to or coming from dates or social engagements. Robbie (and E-Buzz) is also absent as the parents send him away to relatives (oddly in a taxi). The bonds of the family unit are already fraying as Steven's job commitment takes him away from the children for a long period of time—he is performing his duties as the paternal bread-winner of the family but neglecting his duties as a patriarchal father figure, something that is emphasised even more so within the sequel as 'Kane', the human embodiment of the beast, attempts to become a substitute parental figure, who questions Steven's masculinity, ability to provide for his family (emotionally and financially), and his ability to sustain the role of patriarch of the family.

On this intrusion of the environment and incursion into the constructed spaces of the family, George (2006) notes the fissures of the family as they are ripped apart both figuratively and literally. Kellner (1983b) notes that the text provides a positive (without being overtly saccharine in nature) take on the nuclear family dynamic, with Williams (2014) arguing that the antagonists in *Poltergeist* safely project family and social tensions into a demonic protagonist but is flawed by not exploring these key issues in a deeper context due to its convenient love and family conquers all conclusion. While this analysis is justified, and the film does indeed conclude with them having vanquished the intrusion, they have gone through a transformative process brought on by trauma and physical and emotional loss, and the stripping back of the comforts and surroundings of this lifestyle with these personal and economic insecurities are glossed over, and convenient external scapegoats are made without these issues being addressed.

The implication is that the family through the scenario of *Poltergeist* with the loss and return of a child provide the perfect environment to explore the concept of what 'family' means and through interactions and the cathartic processes of grief and joy the family during the finale of the film represents a new, mindful, respectful middle class who have gone through the process of recovery and where normalcy is once again re-established.

While Kellner (1983b) claims that the film's portrayal of a traditional happy family pulling together, surviving disaster, and leaving show that pre-conformity has won over the 'Other', the tangible underlying social, economic, and political issues remain once the supernatural veneer has come off; there is still a threat by an outside influence and the security of home, environment, and living still exist, as is seen within the second film as Steven is reduced to door-to-door sales as the reality of the change in circumstances reveal themselves financially. He is also returning to battle and overcome the fundamental enemy from the original film—the corporatisation of America. While Teague was the face of the corner-cutting and profit-driven real-estate company, Steven still has issues with the faceless corporation driving profits and consumerism as he is shown repeatedly on the telephone during the second film arguing with faceless bureaucracy as he attempts to get payment from the insurance company that is unwilling to take his claim on the grounds that they cannot quantify that the Freeling house has 'gone'—the structure of a pre-conformed, process-driven faceless corporation with no time for detail or circumstances that do not fit a certain criterion; if the claim is not of a pre-determined set of circumstances then they are unwilling to do anything about it. Any deviation from conformity and procedure is rejected (the house is not there, which is evident by the archaeologists in the second film) and the Freelings by not conforming (or having a claim that cannot easily be managed) have themselves become the 'Other'; they are now on the outside of the system and every argument or justification to be let back in and to once again return to normalcy will be rebuffed.

Figure 4.2. Blue-collar intrusion

Williams (2014) argues that *Poltergeist* as a text safely projects family and social tensions into a demonic protagonist, but the film is deeply flawed in exploring these key issues in a deeper context due to its convenient 'love and family conquers all' conclusion. These personal and economic insecurities are glossed over, and convenient external scapegoats are made without these issues being addressed. George and La Manna (2016) also highlight the tensions and fissures within the Freelings as the perfected representation of a 1980s nuclear family, noting that figuratively and literally the family unit and environment in which they dwell are ripped apart.

Chapter 5: Television and trauma

Since the 1950s television has become an everyday piece of household furniture, a significant part of the environmental design of the home; a television is within the 'landscape in the living room' (Burgess, 1987). Within *Poltergeist*'s narrative the television is used as a conduit for the external evasive force from the other side, and the abduction by the 'Other' of a child from a typical American family. Utilising this modern, everyday object in this context heightens the emotional grief and loss inherent in the text; the connection to normality and to the familiar and the implication that the events occurring within the narrative of the film (no matter how wild, supernatural, or uncanny) could, theoretically, happen to the viewer creates an environment of heighted tension and fear in which the viewer identifies with the family. With the familiar setting (practically every home across the Western world has one or multiple televisions) amplifying the sense of unease, fear, and trauma Hooper and Spielberg managed to create a film that lingers in its ability to unnerve.

With *Poltergeist* Hooper and Spielberg purposely set out to extenuate 'the age of television', as screens are always present and on within the film—be that when the children are at breakfast, having friends around to watch the football, or for the family to fall asleep in front of. The ability to stop or avoid the presence of the 'Invasive Other' of the television into the living environment is shown to no longer be possible. In texts such as *Salem's Lot* (1979), *Fright Night* (1985), and *The Lost Boys* (1987), there is a need for the 'Other' (in all cases vampires) to be invited into the safe environment of the home; however, within *Poltergeist* the protagonist and invasive 'Other' is there, already embedded into the family life, hidden in plain site within the very present television.

By the 1980s multiple television sets had entered living spaces and become signifiers of wealth and prestige; television(s) had become an accepted part of the family, an everyday object that had connections to individuals and families. Other films such as *Back to the Future* show the beginning of America's affinity and love for television (as presented in the 1950s sections), and by the early 1980s there was the notion of 'tee-vee' with cable delivering multiple channels to choose from as a bombardment of advertising had become commonplace, with family life now orientated around it.

The television as a main focal point of entry for the 'Other' into this shared family environment is established early on within the narrative. The TV, as with many homes, is part of the dynamic of household life; it is as much a part of the Freelings's environment as the house they live in, the children's bedroom, and the natural bickering and interaction between members of the family. Initially shown as a comfort, a passive box of plastic parts to fall asleep in front of, the representation of television within the narrative evolves to become an active portal to a multitude of other places, times, and experiences. There is no incantation from a book bound in flesh or the unlocking of intricate puzzle boxes to transport the protagonists to a realm of pleasures and pain. The television as a conduit is there and with just a flick of a switch you can go and be part of a crowd at a football game, a voyeur in a battle through the broadcast of a war film, or be comforted in Mr Rogers' Neighbourhood, and if any of those do not take your fancy there is of course hundreds of other options to choose from.

5.1 'THE TV PEOPLE'

The varied semiotic representations of television in film narratives are as wide and varied as the critical theories of genre film studies itself, drawing in discussion based around areas of psychoanalysis, feminism, and social study of broadcast theory. To sum up and conclude the role of television in film it might be best to allow for one of television's most recognised stars (and amateur theorist) Homer Simpson to have his own, very specific opinion on the role and relationship he has with television, describing it as a 'Teacher, Mother, Secret Lover'.

As noted, the initial representation of television in *Poltergeist* is one of a relatable, comfort-providing box of wiring and circuitry that is an integral part of the family environment. This physical presence of television sets and their representation in horror narratives ranges greatly; from its use as a means to mirror, double, or pastiche the initial narratives of films such as *Gremlins* or *Fright Night*, or to become the instigator of intrusion from antagonists in films such as *TerrorVision* (1986) or *Demons 2* (1986) television as a symbol of commentary or gateway to somewhere or something else is used significantly within the horror genres.

POLTERGEIST

Other, more subtle, representations of television within the media have its physicality take the form of an educator, surrogate parent, or to even an unwanted interloper, cuckoo, evil-step mother, or a lover. Spiegel (1992) suggests, 'The television set was often likened to a monster that threatened to wreak havoc on the family.' Other academics and critics such as Graber (1987) have a differing opinion on 1980s cinematic representation of television, stating that coding and representation of television as 'complex', as the audience of a film would both understand the nature of television but in turn take away what they want from what is broadcast on it.

The significance therefore of the continued presence of television and it constantly broadcasting within *Poltergeist* has numerous points of analysis within the text with the first and most significant of these being television's symbolic nature as a device that encapsulates the notion of distilled America consumerism. This representation of a consumer object can be defined in both its physical nature as a 'manufactured product' and the contents that it broadcasts. The notion of bigger is better for the size of the screen highlights the perceived virility of American industrial and manufacturing prowess. While the presentations of dimensions and size of a television are important to represent this notion, equally valid is the presentation of the material created to be used to broadcast. Again the significance of bigger is better is mirrored here as multiple channels are at the consumers' fingertips and in-between Hollywood produced shows adverts are shown to market and promote other goods to consume, all the time reinforcing the need to buy, and to buy American.

While *Poltergeist* presents these discursive themes of television in terms of physical product and its broadcasting matter also highlighted in detail is the personal relationship that the Freelings have with the television. Within the context of the Freeling family, television is presented as being hugely important to the narrative, as it is a device that is continually on, providing background noise, subliminally selling something, or providing news and even at times stark satire on the addiction of children to broadcasting.

Very identifiable American television imagery and motifs are also blatantly used to underpin the narrative—from the appearance of Mr Rogers and the 'big-game' football match to generic war films these are all relatable 'Americanised' images of television that are universally coded to be instantly recognisable to anyone watching—cinematic

73

shorthand to highlight the importance that television plays within a traditional middle-class family. Within the text we also see Hooper's use of television to present satire of America's reliance on consumerism, with the broadcasts shown within the text purposely presented to be brash, bold, and consumer led, a nod to the prowess of television and its all-reigning significance of broadcasting within the home—as the introduction for the *Outer Limits* states, 'We control the horizontal, we control the vertical.'

Figure 5.1. 'The TV people'

The opening scenes of *Poltergeist* focus on what Beebe (1983) describes as an 'ambiguous image, a field of coloureds pulsation', which as the initial credits of the text roll is shown in focus to be the traditional 'closedown' of American television—a familiar montage of images of patriotic Americana that are visually over-laid as 'The Star-Spangled Banner' plays as the day's broadcast comes to an end. As the camera draws back static kicks in and the television is revealed to have been left on as Steven Freeling had fallen asleep in front of it. The initial establishing tracking shot portrays a night-time scene with members of the Freeling family asleep while the television itself is still on, providing pictures, narratives, and messages while those around are 'switched off' and not engaged with the televisual output.

Presenting the television in this way as a continual twenty-four-hour non-stop provider of information and entertainment even when those around need to shut down codes the television as a continual destabilising presence in the home (Weinstock and Lauro, 2017).

POLTERGEIST

Within the film television is used to both provoke and provide excitement within its protagonists, such as the scene showing Steven's friends who are over at the Freelings's house to socialise and watch the football. However, television is also used in such a way to pacify and lull its audience with Carol Anne casually switching on the television in the kitchen and proceeding to sit and stare in front of it, something she has obviously done numerous times before. Frank Lloyd Wright suggests that television is represented as 'chewing gum for the eyes' with most of its content having little or no relationship for its intended purpose, which could arguably be defined by the British Broadcasting Corporation's (within the UK) scope of broadcast content to be material that is 'to educate and inform'. In *Poltergeist* the family's relationship with television is a very close one; there are multiple sets throughout the house and while the initial shots are shown with Steven sleeping in front on a set this scene is coded—being black and white, distorted, inhuman, and artificial—to have no warmth, no heart, and no emotive connection.

Television as a parent or surrogate (actress Nicole Eggert jokingly noted, 'My step-parent was the TV set') is also relevant in the narrative: television is shown repeatedly as an artificial babysitter, which underpins Spielberg's notion that *Poltergeist* can be read as a modern fairy-tale. While not initially inherently evil the television within the narrative does come to encompass a trait of the fairy-tale protagonist, a modernised representation of a wicked stepmother, witch, or Baba Yaga, an entity or person who tricks their way into a home or family with the intent to do harm.

Taking this analogy further, the poltergeists themselves are portrayed as reinterpretations of fey, faeries, or changelings of Germanic folklore, Brothers Grimm stories, or Hans Christian Andersen tales—creatures or supernatural entities that snatch children for their own ends.

The fairy-tale motifs of television are a modern-age device for representing, delivering, or mirroring evil in a similar way that witches, evil queens, or wicked stepmothers would use looking glasses, magic mirrors, or crystals in these original tales—unnatural entities from the 'Other Side'—to watch what their prey is doing and put them under their spell.

When the voices from the 'Other Side' sway, corrupt, and sell, television is framed as a 'Cuckoo'—a parasitic artefact that Mander (1978) describes as an irredeemable menace

DEVIL'S ADVOCATES

that worms its way into human minds, using a home to 'nest', taking over entire aspects of family, removing the host roles from the aspects of nurturing.

Unlike other texts that present television in its physicality, presented as a body, for example, the television with *Poltergeist* does not go through a transformative or metamorphic change; it is coded as a conduit to the 'Other Side', a subliminal communication device that, unlike Cronenberg's representation of television as a living, breathing, pulsating organic thing in *Videodrome* (1983), is a tool for communication to provide content to a receptive complicit audience not a tactile artefact to interact with. The physicality of television is also not bastardised or mutated as they are in texts such as *A Nightmare on Elm Street 3: Dream Warriors* (1987) in which Freddy Krueger used the physicality of a television as resource against his victims and to introduce them to 'prime time'.

Jeffrey Sconce notes that television seems to have the capacity to 'generate (its) own autonomous spirit world' (Sconce, 2000); the television is a conduit, not an object itself that itself is possessed with the poltergeists and Carol Anne uses it to communicate through but not actually take control of the physical form of the set itself, much in the same way that Sadako crawls out of the front of a television in *Ringu/The Ring* (1998) or 'Blipverts' are transmitted to their audience in *Max Headroom* (1985). The television is a delivery method, not an object of horror. This use of television as a transmission device is used in other films with the Silver Shamrock Corporation with *Halloween III* (1982) using a similar method to not only sell but to bewitch and enthral; however, unlike other films such as *Demons 2* (1986) or *Video Dead* (1987), monsters, zombies, or demonic forms do not rise from it but rather more subtly use the nature of televisual transmission to purvey a message and attain the desired effect from their audience.

This presentation of television as a vehicle for transmissions and of a device that relays the silent/ hidden messages from the poltergeists to Carol Anne within the hijacked static allow the dead to successfully broadcast their message, which mirrors exactly what traditional television broadcast intends to do. By the poltergeists sabotaging the transmission they are mimicking the very purposes that television is intended for—to create and engage an audience with broadcast content (programming, infomercials, adverts, and so forth). Ironically, the spirits are more successful in getting their 'message'

POLTERGEIST

out to their audience (of one) with their subtle promotion and key personalised advertising messages telling Carol Anne things only a child would understand. It is ironic that the undead in *Poltergeist* therefore have a lot more success in reaching their target market, engaging their audience, and succeeding in their advertising/consumer goals than a lot of the traditional advertising methods.

This initial manifestation of the poltergeists is of them presenting a 'sales' message that typifies a marketing or sales representative ethos, talking through and engaging with an audience on a personal level, however, the unnatural nature of the message providers is soon revealed and the visage of personable is removed to reveal the unnatural. Once the communication channel is established and their target 'market' engaged and sold the pretences, subtleties and hidden personable messages are disregarded and lost and the break through into our realm by the poltergeists is forceful and inhuman; they are not 'people' but rather semi-formed electric blue ethereal shapes, luminous and translucent, typifying the immaterial projection of the television from where materialises, taking the form with suits, something to be transferred or broadcast over the airwaves by an electrical signal or transmission.

The poltergeists' initial manifestation have no bodies to them, no physicality, and no natural colouration—they are unearthly, alien, and unnatural in both colour and form, mirroring the transmission and static from where they originate from—it is only when they have access to the material physical world that they have potency to use or possess elements (trees, corpses, and so forth) to interact with the environment. This evolution from their immaterial and inorganic electrical/spirit form to physical manifestations shows the spirits relishing in manipulating, mutating, and shaping the natural and organic, developing tendrils, tentacles, and organic-looking mouths that fully embrace a 'Cronenbergian' body horror aesthetic found in texts such as *Videodrome*.

This initial manifestation of the spirits as static and their eventual bursting through the screen as an inhuman blue and white apparition shows that the conduit of the television as a medium to broadcast material is not the calming, relaxing, and pacifying representation initially portrayed in the text. This coding is very quickly turning around from an embraced and loved part of the family environment to an aggressive, artificial, and human-made interloper. The television and static are also purposely presented to have no warmth and the light generated from the screen is harsh and unearthly, having a cold colour temperature in the higher Kelvin range (about 5,000 to 6,000). This state of being unnatural, cold, and inorganic is enhanced even more with strobing effects and even when Carol Anne uses the television as a way of communicating with her family: the audio transmitted for the television is purposely distorted through electronic means to give it a harsh, unnatural, and inhuman quality.

The purposeful enhancements of these unnatural and unearthly elements further reinforce the static on the television as a 'none-place'. Through these depictions, showing a lack of shape, colour, and recognisable natural forms, television static as an unnatural danger is mirrored in other films such as *The Last Broadcast* (1998) and *White Noise* (2005) with the presentation of an 'electric nowhere' and a void of nothingness behind a piece of glass filled with a 'snow-blind oblivion' from which viewers might not ever escape (Sconce, 2000). This innate fear of a viewer tricked or abducted, taken away to a place that could forever trap you behind glass with no means of escape, is a horror trope that plays into modern fears, much in the same way as the 'invasion, replacement or cohesion into a collective' message that is prevalent within the paranoia-focused body-snatching horror of the 1950s and 1960s.

The depiction of this modern horror trope by Hooper and Spielberg as to the implied danger of the omnipotent presence of television within the safety of a family environment makes this perceived safe space for children into one that is now unsafe. With consumers happily inviting the influence of television into the home both producer and director vilify the presence of television and imply its influence upon American culture and American youth as being far too controlling and influential— whereas the *Invaders from Mars* took over and replaced individuals so too does television with the viewer encouraged, influenced, or even brainwashed into the commercial and consumer culture that television requires to sustain itself—proving the point that too much television will inevitably hurt the viewer's eyes.

5.2 Mirror, mirror

Within the film the 'Other' presented as the poltergeists interject themselves into the family through the conduit of a television set, both destabilising the family unit and

POLTERGEIST

the status quo of the family's environment, lifestyle, and hierarchy. As such, with the established family structure unable to cope with this interjection there is a requirement for them to gain external agency and experience to interject to provide support and guidance.

This first call to action is triggered by Steven Freeling, whose initial request for help comes from the instigation of 'employing' a university parapsychologist team led by Doctor Lesh. This move to external help and to gain assistance from authority and experts in this field (there are, of course, no real 'experts' in parapsychology until *Ghostbusters* in 1984!) shows a team still reliant on conventional methods and rationality to quantify the abduction of Carol Anne. The reliance on technology (and enthusiasm) to counteract the antagonist's influences is initially sceptical in nature, however, while Doctor Lesh and her team are eventually convinced the team's agency for change is limited and while they appear helpful, they are ultimately not expert enough or have enough convincing authority to be able to provide any serious assistance to something far removed from conventional logic and conventions.

The paranormal investigators are represented in the same contexts of consumerism and the material as the Freelings themselves; while the Freelings have adorned their home with material goods Doctor Lesh's team's equally impressive display of paraphernalia, equipment, and physical tangible materials (cameras, monitors, and recording equipment) show again an Americanised display of 'bigger is better'. The vast equipment and set-up they bring with them mirrors the abundance of gadgetry and consumer goods that the affluent, consumer-driven, middle-class Freelings have within their home. The cluttering up and sharing the space with more audio and video equipment and televisions, for example, provide additions to the already existing impressive amount of home entertainment systems (again televisions) installed within their house. Steven even tells his boss Teague that the team's audio-visual collection is part of his hobby, a lie to cover for the paranormal investigation that is outside the scope of middle-class normalcy but is believable enough within the context of the narrative due to the over-abundance of consumer goods that already fill the Freelings's living space.

This reliance on modern material goods allows the spirits within the texts to attack the investigators in the same way they have already tormented the family but to an even harsher extent. Unlike the Freelings, who up until this point have not been physically harmed by the poltergeists (it is debatable if Robbie was going to be swallowed by the tree), the external assistance the team provides provokes and antagonises the poltergeists who are much more aggressive with Marty becoming the focal point for the physical attacks.

Initially bitten by something unseen Marty is shown to have large physical aggression focused on him. Within the screenplay and novel this attack is expanded on, and his aggressor shown in more detail (it is described as a variant of the 'Door Guardian'). While Marty is not portrayed in the text as a bad or evil character his personality traits are seen within the text as negative with aspects of cynicism, greed, and arrogance highlighted. As such, his negative aspects are reproached, initially for not believing in the 'power' antagonists wield and then for his lack of authority and agency—he is a character portrayed not without knowledge but not wise, lacking emotional intelligence and empathy for the family. This lack of empathy and blasé nature is shown by his easily distractive nature and his enthrallment by material goods, sating his personal well-being over that of the family. This self-serving nature is highlighted through the scene where at night his quest for self-fulfilment leads him to take without permission the Freelings's goods (food). While there is no malice, subterfuge, and no outright stealing he is not seen to ask or be given permission to take something—again showing the continued underpinning of his childlike and self-serving behavioural traits present in the text (and even more so within the novel).

With this transgressive behaviour of eating the chicken from the fridge and planning and prepping to eat the steak (a symbol of wealth) taking place and being found out and caught not by the Freelings but by the poltergeists they provide a punishment for his actions of taking without asking—a very 'traditional' story trope used in fairy tales, myths, and legends.

It is with this transgression of stealing that leads to one of the most grotesque and extreme scenarios of the whole film—the infamous bathroom mirror/face-ripping scene that is both repulsive and fascinating. While the physical effects may well have suffered a little with age (although are still very unnerving) the set-up and execution of Marty's punishment still has the power to shock and repulse.

POLTERGEIST

This is abject horror in the extreme, a fairy-tale tradition of 'who is the fairest of them all' inverted with the 'magic mirror' (represented as an ordinary bathroom mirror) showing back at the viewer the most grotesque and horrific image, a self-reflected horror to provide revulsion and extreme emotional response.

Figure 5.2. Horror in the mirror

The scene, although violent and repulsive, is ambiguous and does not answer the question of whether what Marty is seeing in the mirror is really happening to him, an illusion, or a reflection of how he sees himself. He is reflected as a skinless distorted double, an embodiment of un-surmounted supernaturalism (Gentile, 2000) that marks another eruption of the 'uncanny' and supernatural into the everyday believable context of the film.

This scene presents another movement away from the film's representation of rational and quantifiable fears and of the 'corporeal reality' (Carol Anne moving across the floor, which could be attributed to magnetism, earthquakes, or electrical static from the storm) into one filled with the supernatural, illusion, and the uncanny. This personalised dismantling of reality presents a breakdown for Marty in both physical and conceptual ways. The scene, in all its grotesquery, provides an example of 'abjection'—a term used to describe the distinction between what is self and what is the 'Other' and that from which immediately could threaten one's sense of life (Kristeva, 1980).

DEVIL'S ADVOCATES

The traditional use of mirrors within the context of narrative (specifically 'fantastical' texts) depicts them as an instrument used for 'scrying', fortune-telling voyeurism, or spying on others—used by the Witch of the West in *The Wizard of Oz* to watch over Dorothy's actions, for example. The other representation of mirrors in this context is for the notion of self-assurance or vanity in the case of Snow White's stepmother to know 'who is the fairest of them all'. In the context of poltergeists' representation of mirrors, specifically in this harrowing bathroom scene suggestion of fairest of them all is inversed with the reflection Marty seeing not being one that returns beauty but rather a reflection that portrays extreme ugliness and horror (Shengold, 1974), which the poltergeists force upon him to confront.

What Marty and the viewers as voyeurs see in this mirror could therefore be interpreted as all his character and personal faults and insecurities made physical, something that underpins Freudian and Rank theories that suggest a 'double' reflected from a mirror of what an individual perceives to be him or herself—a true image of their nature presented as a transformed 'personal' perception of their own humanity. This notion of viewing one's true self through reflection by using an artefact such as an enchanted 'mirror' is suggested by Myers (2017) to be an attempt by Marty to find a 'true' self—and that through the poltergeist influenced/possessed mirror he is allowed and given permission to reveal his own nature through literally ripping away at his own face , gouging and peeling back his own skin in an attempt to reveal this perceived notion of self underneath. This self-harm and removal of the skin to find the 'true you' is seen in other films, with Clive Barker's *Nightbreed* (1990) showing the character Narcisse attempting to pull off his own face to reveal his 'true' hidden self.

This scene is one of the most physically intense elements of the film, its gratuitous and gory nature nearly gaining the film an 'R' rating in the United States, with Spielberg having to argue that the scene was a hallucination and therefore not 'real'. For these deeper assumptions of self-reflective analysis to truly work, a criticism could be levelled at the film in that the narrative might have established the character's more negative traits and nature in more detail. While Marty is a secondary character these issues of self-doubt (in the hierarchy of investigators he is the least experienced) could have been emphasised to a greater extent. The character is not initially coded as inherently bad, antagonistic, 'evil', or malicious compared to the major antagonists of the film, both natural (the building company) and unnatural (The Beast), and, as such, while the reading of these scenes could conclude that this still unnerving episode is an illusion first and foremost, it's also suggestive of a trick taken too far, a very nasty sense of humour of a naughty child taken to extremes. This scene tells us that the 'fun and games' tactics the spirts have been using are over, replaced with malicious and malevolent cruelty. 'Marty will not be coming back,' as Lesh puts it, and indeed, like Marty, the previously playful tone of the film is essentially written out of the narrative from that point onwards.

CHAPTER 6: MATRIARCHY AND MONSTERS—THE IMPORTANCE OF FAMILY AND THE FEMININE

Reading *Poltergeist* from a feminine critical perspective presents a text that displays a wide range of strong, well-written female characters who provide both critical roles and agency for change within the narrative, an issue that had arguably been lacking in both Spielberg's and Hooper's prior works.

6.1 THE 'EVERY-WOMAN' HEROINE

Representations of positive femininity and strong female characters in both Hooper's and Spielberg's prior works are considered limited; female characters within both auteurs' previous cinematic repertoire are portrayed typically with little or no power on screen. Both directors' depiction of female characters had been typically shown to have no authority above and beyond those of established matriarchal roles personified and coded as wives and mothers to the point of even being reduced to a supportive role or narrative device that allowed the progression of the 'everyman' protagonists. Potency of the female characters as agents of change and authority are near non-existent, especially within Spielberg's prior narratives of his 'Suburban Trilogy'. The Ronnie Neary role in *Close Encounters*, for example, becomes almost redundant within the film's final act as she provides very little in the way of resistance in stopping her husband leaving. This lack of female characterisation coded with no agency for change is also evident within the narrative of *E.T.* with Dee Wallace's character Mary also showing little to no power in presenting or providing resistance against the authorities in taking Elliot away, providing little more in that role above and beyond that of being a competent maternal head of the family.

With Tobe Hooper's prior films, his presentation of strong female characters do not fair a great deal better in their characterisation and agency for changes with his most famous 'final girl' Sally Hardesty presented in *The Texas Chain Saw Massacre* not as a heroine but rather as the sole survivor of Leatherface and his family within the film. She is both physically battered and psychologically broken and in no way is she presented

85

DEVIL'S ADVOCATES

as the hero/heroine of the piece surviving the monstrous encounter and eventually escaping the family but is neither shown 'slaying the beast' nor overcoming the very masculine all-male antagonists of the Sawyers' clan.

Within *Poltergeist*, however, the atypical 'Spielbergian' two-dimensional matriarchal stereotypes are replaced by much more rounded representations of female characters and show a maturity and equality to the gender dynamics with the film presenting several strong authoritarian female portrayals and perspectives on screen and is a far better representation of second-wave feminism and equality than a large number of female-driven or female-led narratives of the time.

Diane Freeling is not a typical protagonist, neither initially coded as the typical resourceful young female role nor the Clover-esque 'Final Girl', but something else, which as Arnold (2013) suggests is more of the 'good mother' figure, a role in which she is having to take charge of the well-being of the family unity rather than just her individual survival.

Diane is represented as an attractive, young, free-spirited, home-maker—combining both motherly attributes and parental responsibilities with vibrant enthusiasm and open-mindedness. Whereas Steven has near fully conformed to the rationality and contemporary 'mature' conservative Reagan-esque values of the suburban environment, Diane, while adopting these traits of homemaker, still presents aspects of a free-spirted, open-minded, non-conforming individual yet to be fully integrated in the collective. Surrounded by the vast housing estate presentation of repetition and stifling conformity she exudes individual elements of a free-spirited nature, willing to flush away problems of dead pets when nobody is watching, smoking pot in bed, and associating and interacting with working-class/blue-collar workers who could be seen to be 'below' her current social standing. This non-conformity, free will, and agency are what promotes her to advocate her daughter's rebuttal from the builders in her employ to build the swimming pool and what takes her further into realms of the uncanny in her positive belief in the spirits as they move Carol Anne around the kitchen.

Her positive feminine outlook opposes the restrictions of the family environment and pre-established roles and coding of the 'housewife', 'doting mother', or passive female antagonist and while never assuming the identity of 'hero' in the film she is the one

86

that undergoes the trials of the Hero's Journey to evolve as a character to become the 'heroine' and significant agent for change.

Figure 6.1. Diane Freeling, the heroine

Having Diane as a 'good mother' character shows her not as a stereotypical action hero/heroine role model but one who has to still successfully traverse the 'Campbellian' hero's journey to achieve her objective and complete her quest (in this case to retrieve her daughter Carol Anne from the 'Other Side') and is transformed both physically and emotionally from this event via the notion of 'The American Monomyth' (Lawrence and Jewett, 1977), eventually ending up with much more in common in terms of her actions and attitudes to the likes of empowered female heroines such as Leia Organa, Ellen Ripley, and Sarah Conner than the likes of Laurie Stroud or Nancy Thompson who surviving their ordeal did not evolve through their trauma within the narrative of the initial film's plot, a point that becomes mute due to the notions of horror narratives' inevitable sequels presenting heroines who return mature, empowered, and taking on a new dynamic (mentor, antagonist, equal) within these texts.

It is Diane whose sole endeavours, resourcefulness, and material instincts are tested through the set of 'Campbellian' trials that ultimately saves the family, while Steven, the

DEVIL'S ADVOCATES

patriarchal figure of the family has to allow his empowered 'equal' (a point highlighted between themselves just before Diane is instructed to go through the portal to the 'Other Side') to take the risk and enter the 'Abyss' and be transformed where he is stuck, getting no further than the 'Threshold'.

This inability for Steven to progress through the 'Hero's Journey' cycle could be seen as a punishment, his quest failing due to a prior transgression. It could be debated that while not directly responsible for the trauma brought on to the family by the poltergeists he is unintentionally implicit in their actions due to his association with the real-estate company who are the catalyst for the initial problems and trauma the family ultimately face due to the profit and materialist driven goals that involve cost cutting and shoddy work by only removing the gravestones and not the actual graves that sit below the Freeling house.

Both Steven and to a greater extent Teague, the most significant representations of masculinity of the film, are left out of the quest and moved to the boundaries while others successfully take centre stage. It is Diane's journey to the 'Other Side' to rescue Carol Anne and successfully complete her trail that eventually provides her with her rewards of reuniting with her daughter as well as being the one that 'spiritually restores' the emotional bonds between the family members, providing the catalyst for the evolution of the whole family unit, whose rejection of the negative cycle of consumerism represented within the film creates a new dynamic for the family based more on mindfulness and compassion rather than credit cards and conformity.

6.2 REPRESENTATIONS OF FEMININE AUTHORITY

Diane's journey to the 'Other Side' to rescue Carol Anne sees the restoration of both the emotional bonds between the family and a return to the established patriarchal hierarchy that typifies the 'nuclear family' stereotype. To attain this re-established status quo, however, there is a requirement within the narrative for the characters to move beyond the typified norms of authority that allow for individuals to attain certain levels of agency at specific junctures of the film but for them to be superseded by those who are more qualified to the tasks at hand. As the family members move into realms, they

POLTERGEIST

cannot comprehend that those with more knowledge and agency are needed, which include those whose boundaries of what becomes the 'norm' differ significantly from that of a traditional family unit.

The initial hierarchy of the family presents Steven taking the role of the authority figure (being the patriarch of the house)—where he provides both emotive and financial support for the family—but he does not represent a dominating male figure with little in the narrative supporting the evidence that his pre-designed role is superior to that of Diane who is mother, housewife, and equal.

Steven is never presented as on overtly dominating authoritative figure, and the homicidal patriarch stereotype is never established within the narrative of the film. It is through debate with Diane, his peer within the family, that it is revealed that he is the disciplinarian but only by a margin and that corporate discipline has been issued to the children but rarely. He is neither Jack Torrance in *The Shining* nor George Lutz in *The Amityville Horror*, and the sub-text of an abusive father role is not apparent within the film (although does appear in the sequel).

This duality of responsibility and authority and lack of male-dominated hierarchy make for an interesting dynamic, as Steven is represented not within an overtly masculine role but more within the realms of rationality, logic, science, and the quantifiable, with an example of this being his matter-of-fact explanation to Robbie about lightning and thunder presented in a way that a child understands but dealing with the tangible and real. While Steven represents the material and definable Diane's role as matriarch is one more aligned with the emotive, spiritual, and empathic, being the only one to feel and smell Carol Anne when she touches her soul from the other side. This representation of the two differing roles, outlooks, and representations of the practical/spiritual personas of Steven and Diane mirror the other numerous dualities of the film, such as the juxtaposition of a brand new haunted house, the modernisation of traditional folklore, and the technical and metaphysical representation of the 'Other Side' (not to mention the two endings, or debateable directors of the film) and allows Steven agency to be more practical in responses to the events and eventually allowing for Diane and the feminine to align more with the requirements to counteract the masculine entity represented by 'The Beast'.

89

DEVIL'S ADVOCATES

While the antagonists within the text are shown to be calculating and intelligent, the Freelings themselves are also shown to be thoughtful and rational in facing a situation outside their sphere and realms of understanding. Putting trust in pre-structured authority can be seen in other texts, with *The Exorcist* (1973) an example of where both the physical and metaphysical establish a hierarchy within a 'real world' recognisable structure to deal with the demon, to 'cure' the possessed child Reagan both physically and spiritually.

The initial analytical investigation of the parapsychologists, including the hi-tech equipment, is of a modern mind-set, tackling a problem using method, calculation, and reason to attempt to quantify the unreasonable within the realms of the material and is coded as masculine (a lot of cameras, audio equipment, and electronics). The reliance on reason and modern technology and trial/error shares a lot in common with *The Entity*, where another malevolent spirit is analysed and eventually attempted to be captured by scientific means, primarily defined as spirts or ghosts—there is no pre-defined higher authority to deal with this type of antagonist (until *Ghostbusters*).

The inadequate nature of pre-defined authority in *Poltergeist* is even debated by Doctor Lesh who admits to not fully comprehending the context they are working in and her fear of the forces that the Freelings are dealing with. For all her qualifications, even those assigned authority and agency lack of comprehension and understanding of the situation.

> Parapsychology isn't something you master in. There are no certificates of graduation. No licenses to practice. I am a professional psychologist who spent most of my time engaged in this ghostly hobby, which makes me I suppose the most irresponsible woman of my age that I know…I'm absolutely terrified. It's all the things that we don't understand. I feel like the proto-human coming out of the forest primeval and seeing the moon for the first time and throwing rocks at it.

As this path towards a more spiritual resolution towards the rescue of Carol Anne becomes apparent the maturity and authority of the female characters grow and the requirement for material (technology, cameras, and equipment) and for male assistance and support diminished. After Steven's initial action to ask for external help from Doctor Lesh and her team (who are not in the *Yellow Pages*) the representation of the positive masculine within the narrative diminishes. As the female character's agency increases with Lesh having power and authority over her research fellows Marty and Ryan (displayed as non-authoritative power as no real hierarchy of their working relationships is established, but it is implied that Lesh is the de-facto leader and head researcher in this area) there is still some reliance on the masculine as she is dependent on her co-workers—not for emotional support but instead less emotive and functional needs with issues like technical or research support. While this support hierarchy has less emotional support than the Freelings as a family there is connection with the mature female dynamic evolving into management rather than parental systems; they are a team, each providing a function and purpose.

Within the team there is also a reliance on the more physical—with two males making up this unit there is evidence of the doubling of the need of the physical material. Whereas the Freelings have the house and the items within it are balanced to the family dynamic to assist in emotional support (the house is a very consumer-centric space) the male-dominant research team encroach on the space with more representations of the masculine with an abundance of video cameras and sensors. With so much 'equipment' on display there is both a signifier of the presentation of masculinity and the need for the team to prove their virility and validity as authority.

However, for all the material goods on show the scope and scale of the poltergeists goes beyond the material into the realms of the spiritual and once again feminine expertise is seen to grow exponentially to counter the menace of the negative masculine, which becomes more aggressive, bestial, and inhuman as finally when we are introduced to Tangina. Appearing at the Freeling house alone, initially not spotted at all, she appears with no masculine support mechanisms, no physical accruements (apart from oversized sunglasses), and no pre-conceptions of pre-existing hierarchies challenging Steven's masculine authority within seconds of meeting him. She is alone and comes with very little in terms of physical prowess (and of course her purposely divisive diminutive stature) but provides agency.

With defining Doctor Lesh and her team as looking at the boundaries of understanding the notion of to 'add to the sum of knowledge' this too has to go out of the bounds of normality. She is presented as a maternal figure and provides a level of authoritative discourse in 'the telling of the tale', explaining the definitions and concepts and the realms of the spiritual to Robbie. The representation of Tangina, therefore, can be as bizarre as possible (Fuery, 2003). By the final acts of the film the definitions and the realms of normalcy have been reconfigured to allow the viewer to believe in the spiritual and allows for Tangina to presented to be as far removed from traditional authoritative figures as possible; she is not the 'norm' and as such has no reliance on family, technology, or other support mechanisms to provide her agency. Her appearance, demeanour, and attitude in circumnavigating social transgressions (she is rude) are purposely done, making her absurdness within the narrative a way of representing the impossible. Tangina relies on intuition and other pre-scientific methods for combatting The Beast with traditional old-fashioned tactics of honesty, understanding, and empathy prevailing over the technology-based tactics, demonstrating once again that a respectful connection with the past is necessary to heal the damage done by the urbanisation, burying of history and context, and the disregard for that which has come before.

Figure 6.2. Female hierarchy

The feminine and female relationship and hierarchy supersede the masculine, both in the physical world and in that of the 'Other Side' when dealing with the spiritual and metaphysical. Diane is young and attractive, Doctor Lesh has embraced her age and social status, whereas Tangina in her appearance is intentionally provocative to create

POLTERGEIST

a reaction and, as Arnold (2013) suggests, the masculine has lost contact with this side, allowing for the feminine to deal within the realms of maternal horror and non-symbolic space.

While this representation of the feminine being more attuned to the spiritual encompasses the majority of Carol Anne's rescue there is still an underlying grounded logic presented; experiments and tests are done, and discussions are held to find the best solution. For horror, this use of scientific theory and clear-minded debate especially dealing with the notion of supernatural or spirit entities shows that neither is more dominant than the other and that the harmony of the relationship of Steven and Diane as equals represents that qualities for both are needed to reunite their family.

The power, family hierarchy, and authority of this is discussed in the scene when they are rescuing Carol Anne and a debate occurs as to who provides discipline, an outcome of which is never really resolved, concluding that authority of the couple is shared by both, something that is significant in the return and reuniting of the family unit.

In conclusion, while it is those more attuned to the spiritual who explore and enter the feminine metaphysical space defeating the negative masculine that resides within it is the return to the material (masculine) through a feminine action of birthing that rescues both Diane and Carol Anne. There is a need for both feminine and masculine, spiritual and the physical and a restored balance of both within the narrative with harmony for the family (for a time at least) only achieved with the duality of both male and female acting together, the most spiritually attuned character using scientific language when people are 'jamming her frequencies'.

6.3 BIRTH AND REBIRTH

One of the key factors that provides *Poltergeist* potency to instil fear within its audience is its highly effective use of the 'Other' as an aggressive and intrusive violating presence into a family environment, breaking apart loved ones and separating support structures and maternal mother/child bonds. Having The Beast coded as male throughout the film intentionally creates a scenario where the poltergeists abduct Carol Anne and then he wilfully 'keeps her close', denying this maternal bond to continue putting 'him' at odds

DEVIL'S ADVOCATES

with the potent female characters in the film (Diane, Doctor Lesh, and Tangina) over the custody and dominion of Carol Anne.

The Beast's interest in Carol Anne and her pure 'virginal' light is never implied to be overtly sexual but rather contextualised to be a requirement of her clean, pure positive energy, with her life-force (and implied supernatural abilities) being the thing that converted to keep the rest of the spirts in the hierarchical nature of the 'Other Side'. This control, domination, and forcefulness of restriction and restraint are again very male in their coding—The Beast is the largest, most imposing spectre in the film and his (or its) physicality is the thing that drives the initial abduction as well as being the barrier that stops the family, especially the female members of the family, from rescuing Carol Anne and reuniting the family both in the closet scene and also within the second attempt to abduct the children.

While the poltergeists in the film initially manifest though modern technology there is a purposeful sterility to them through using signals, static, and 'white noise' to communicate, suggesting that the 'Other Side' is a realm that has no physicality to it and a place filled with cold static blue light, a place of no depth, warmth, or humanity and those residing there themselves are also immaterial and ethereal.

It is only when the spirits break through to this reality that the manifestation of the spiritual becomes tangible. The notion of spirits materialising via ectoplasm has been part or the 'science' of parapsychology since Victorian times and of course played upon to a great extent by *Ghosbusters* in which Venkmen is 'slimed' to an excessive extent. The clean, sterile unnatural blue invoked from the television static of the previous manifestations are replaced by the 'unclean' images in the attempted recapture of Carol Anne via an 'inverse birth' through a corrupt womb visualised through an organic gaping maw filled with tentacles.

These representations of the organic and the themes of birth and rebirth are also evident in the initial rescue of Carol Anne from the 'Other Side' that sees both her and Diane covered in vivid pink material and viscous liquid—supernatural amniotic fluid with mother cradling daughter in a nurturing position. Other imagery associated with birthing are also used in this scene as the mother and daughter are rushed away from the actual birth site and placed into the bath of water and there is the checking for breathing.

Other visual codes from traditional births are also used with the 'hot water and towels' motif used to remove 'afterbirth' with finally the family left alone by Doctor Lesh to 'bond' with their reborn infant and in turn strengthening of bond between the mother/daughter relationship via this rebirthing process.

This abundance of birth and rebirth imagery is also underpinned by comments made by Steven and Diane stating that Carol Anne was born in that house—which again provides evidence of this birth/rebirth motif while also adding to the continued notions of duality and paradox presented in the film.

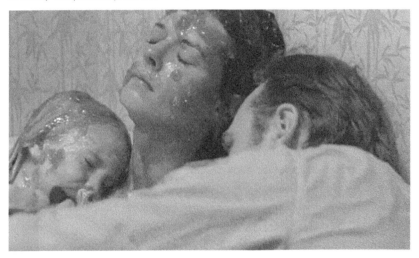

Figure 6.3. Birth and rebirth

6.4 TRANSGRESSION AGAINST THE FEMININE

In Diane's attempt to rescue her children she is subject to physical, emotional, and psychological trauma at the hands of the poltergeist, one that is very much coded as physical male domination of the female. However, this attempted subjugation and the transgressive behaviours towards the female characters is not just via the unseen supernatural entries in the climax of the film but is a theme that is intertwined through the entire narrative.

One of the most obvious and quite unsettling initial objectifications of female characters within the text is by the 'blue collar' workmen digging the family's pool. While their none-too-subtle sexual advances could be contextualised as being seen to be made in jest, she is nonetheless objectified, and it is obvious that by wearing a school uniform she is still arguably under the age for consent (she is stated to be 16). Four decades on, this scene feels in bad taste and disquieting. The uncomfortable nature is further enhanced by Diane's reaction, a maternal figure who passively accepts and allows this objectification of her daughter to occur, even to go as far as to smile at her daughter's retort.

While this initial objectification of Dana is obvious and while further minor actions and comments made by the character do imply she is indeed sexually active, the narrative proceeds without this character's involvement for significant periods of time with her involvement becoming secondary to the driving-plot points of losing Carol Anne and the attempts to retrieve her.

As such the focus of implied objectification is Diane and while her character is never intentionally coded to be overtly sexualised there are numerous occasions where she becomes subject to objectification, as per Mulvey's theory of the 'male-gaze' (1975). She is an attractive young mother signifying Diane as an *object of desire* and as such objectifies the heroine of the narrative superseding both the established role as matriarch and the main female protagonist of the film. Diane's objectification ranges from very passive to highly aggressive, reinforcing her femininity that she is still sexually desirable, still sexually active (as implied in the bedroom scene where Diane and Steven are rolling a joint), and still has potency and agency within the realms of feminine power, which is utilised within the film rather than receding into the stereotype of cinematic motherhood.

One of the initial objectifications and 'male-gaze' of the female character comes when Diane and Carol Anne are 'playing' with the poltergeist with Carol Anne being pulled across the floor. While the film is set in a balmy summer in California this scene fetishises Diane as she wears tight shorts and trainers bringing attention to and accentuating her tanned, uncovered legs.

POLTERGEIST

This overt sexualisation of Diane is played to an even greater extent in the climax of the film where there is implication that she is assaulted by the coded masculine force of the poltergeist. After Carol Anne has been rescued and the family are reunited in the 'clean' house the poltergeists create a final attempt to recapture Carol Anne. In doing this the spirits become a sexual and physical threat to Diane in her own bedroom, the place where she ought to feel the most secure. In the scene she is stopped from attempting to rescue both Robbie and Carol Anne from a new attack and she is pinned to the bed, signifying greatly non-consensual, aggressive, physical force used that verges on sexual abuse. Represented as mindless, angry, and forceful the poltergeist forgoes any pretence of subtlety and is presented as a very base/primal and male aggressor—presenting what it is in its most basic form, a mindless 'Beast'. As Diane is involuntarily dragged up the wall the assault and restraint continue in a gravity-defying manner, upturning Diane onto the celling of her room (the initial script is more explicit in the description of this scene—a special harness to imitate 'rape' movements was scrapped when the idea endangered the picture's PG rating). An alternate scene of Jo-Beth Williams writhing in bed remains, its darker implications less apparent (Suskin, 1982) In a filmed scene, the hole in the master bedroom also grows a spider-like array of tentacles that grab Diane instead of the finished shot of the invisible 'manhandling' she receives. This resemblance to an unseen and invisible violator is like one within the contemporaneous *The Entity*, in which invisible 'male' also hands abuse to Barbara Hershey's character Carla Moran.

This assault by the masculine 'Beast' along with other male objectifications used against Diane within the finale, the vicious 'Door Guardian', the erection of the graves though the floor, and the grabbing, clamouring hands of the skeletons are all attempts by the male-coded spirits to physically stop or violate Diane, showing vain attempts to physically stop her but also an intent to stop the reconnection of the mother/daughter dynamic, a metaphorical supernatural custodial battle for the children where every attempt is made to stop the female side of the family reuniting. However, it is with empowered aspects of femininity she has enhanced through the 'transformation' stages of her quest (such as a desired loving partner and a loving, providing, maternal mother) and finally through the 'resurrection/rebirth' stage that she overcomes these final attempted violations and shows agency to not only survive her heroine's journey but excels and gain her reward (Carol Anne) to finally attempt to complete the cycle and return to the beginning of the journey once again—one framed within the notion of a 'normal' life.

Chapter 7: Cultural resonance and conclusions

Poltergeist is a film of somewhat convoluted and murky production history in which those ancillary debates surrounding the text are deeply intertwined with its cinematic legacy. While *Poltergeist* as a film succeeds without these additional layers of context via its strong script, relatable characters, and a cohesive world-building mythology, even four decades after the film's original release the film's 'meta-narrative' still provides themes for discussion and debate.

7.1 The direction of the film

The history of the directorial credit surrounding the film is rich and varied, providing evidence of claims and counter-claims that are notably fully of contradictory elements. In a written *L.A. Times*' piece released in 1982 Spielberg states that he would frequently lead creative discussions, implying that Hooper often deferred to him. Hooper, in turn, quoted in Pollock (1982), comments, 'I directed the film and I did fully half of the story boards.' This in turn contradicts producer Frank Marshall, who claims Hooper handed in his cut of the film on 17 October 1981 and was subsequently hardly involved in any directorial decisions or post-production work until he screened the movie on 17 April 1982.

Spielberg and Marshall have denied that Hooper was not allowed access to or control of the film at any stage during the movie's production. Spielberg even decried the notion in 1982, saying that the situation of directorial credit had been 'misunderstood'. Hooper also provides an explanation mirroring these comments, stating in an interview with Bob Martin with Fangoria (1982), '*Poltergeist* will always be a tricky movie. Several people who should have gotten credit, didn't get credit. There's a lot of magic and business mysticism connected with it. We're all still trying to figure this one out.'

On the 25th anniversary of the film, Hooper told reporters from A.V. Club that the whole issue with the directorial credits was just a giant misunderstanding brought on by the *L.A. Times*' article, noting:

DEVIL'S ADVOCATES

The genesis of it came from an article in The L.A. Times: When we were shooting the practical location on the house, the first two weeks of filming were exterior, so I had second-unit shots that had to be picked up in the front of the house... The L.A. Times arrived on the set and printed something like, 'We don't know who's directing the picture.' The moment they got there, Steven was shooting the shot of the little race cars, and from there the damn thing blossomed on its own and started becoming its own legend. (Tobias, 2007)

Others have differing views, however, with Buckland (2006) suggesting that Tobe Hooper had very little in the way of directorial input into the film and he was in a literal sense a 'ghost director'. Keller (1983a), however, notes that the film exhibits 'Hooper's flair for the suspenseful, odd, and horrific and Spielberg's affection for the middle-class, fuzzy-minded occultism'. McBride (1987) argues that Spielberg's involvement on Poltergeist was 'unusually intense for a producer and writer... It was generally believed in Hollywood that Spielberg simply moved in and took over the film creatively.'

Dennis Giles conclusively states that 'Tobe Hooper is the director of record, but Poltergeist is clearly controlled by Steven Spielberg'; however, the direction of the piece has more in common with Robert Latham's take on the more complex relationship between producer/director commenting that Poltergeist is 'an uneasy alliance between Spielberg's confidence in the suburban project and Hooper's corrosive contempt for bourgeois institutions'. To oppose this view, according to Waller (1987) Spielberg controlled the film, citing the film's upbeat ending and the fact that the demonic has been dispatched and displaced, which mirrors a lot of the director's other work of 'happy-ever-after' conclusions. Muir (2002, 2013) provides a more pragmatic theory that Poltergeist was the creative vision of dual directors—one whose focus was on satire (Hooper) and one whose focus was on sincerity (Spielberg), concluding that the directorial credit should go to both Hooper and Spielberg. This is supported by the evidence within the narrative that while the Freelings escape their life their world view has been compromised. As such normalcy is not fully restored; there is no return to their original status quo caused by the events in the film.

In an interview for Blumhouse and Fangoria 'Shockwaves' podcast (2017), director John Leonetti asserted that Poltergeist was directed by Spielberg rather than Hooper.

Explaining that his brother cinematographer Matt Leonetti was the director of photography of *Poltergeist* and was on set for every single shot of the film, he states: 'There's a lot going on. And candidly...Steven Spielberg directed that movie.'

This revelation is also backed up by a statement provided by actress Zelda Rubinstein (who played Tangina Barrons): 'I can tell you that Steven directed all six days I was there. I only worked six days on the film and Steven was there. Tobe set up the shots and Steven made the adjustments.' It is with these continued revelations that the controversy surrounding the directorial credit for *Poltergeist* still endures. While Leonetti's statement initially seems like a 'conclusive' end to the debate these comments muddy the water even further, contradicting prior statements from both Spielberg and Hooper themselves.

There is enough evidence within *Poltergeist* to read the film as both a 'Hooperian' and 'Spielbergian' text with both lines of debates providing evidence of the purposeful disruption of the white, middle-class 'American' way of life, transgressive behaviour by an 'unseen' antagonist (be that the 'supernatural' and the 'corporate' antagonist) and the detriment that these actions cause the protagonists.

It is doubtful that audiences will ever receive a true and accurate account of the allocation of works on-set of the film on a day-to-day basis, or even if one vision of the film supersedes the other. And while critics and academics still debate the creative process and nature of the partnership between Spielberg and Hooper, *Poltergeist* as a narrative piece works best when both creative forces come into synchronicity. The 'meta-narrative' of *Poltergeist* is one that is still evolving and is far from over, as the continued presentations of new evidence from the film's 'troubled' production and the reframing of the text from a social commentary standpoint can still provide an abundance of critical study of both the narrative subtexts and meta-textual themes presented by the film.

7.2 CRITICAL ANALYSIS

The film's legacy still influences music and television decades later and there is continual reference in popular culture. The Chicago Film Critics Association noted that it is 'one of the scariest films ever made' (Soares, 2014), and the American Film Institute (AFI, 2001)

DEVIL'S ADVOCATES

put the film in its list of the top '100 years, 100 thrills' list. Writing for *The New York Times*, critic Vincent Canby notes that the film is a 'marvellously spooky ghost story' while Peter Rainer (1982), writing for the *L.A. Herald Examiner*, states that *Poltergeist* was 'a basic, splendid fairy tale...Virtually all fairy tales begin with a disrupting of the family order, and their conclusion is usually a return to order.'

The 'power' of a family facing adversity is a repeated motif and theme for Spielberg works with Gordon (2008) noting that the director's 'suburban' trio of texts (*Close Encounters, E.T.,* and *Poltergeist*) are just three versions of the same film. There is a repetition of themes of abandonment, the unknown, suspicion of authority, and outside forces beyond the control of the family unit essentially repurposed to fit differing narratives. James and Berg (1996) note that both *E.T.* and *Poltergeist* present an insertion of an external force or 'Other' into a pre-established family environment but with *E.T.* the audience is provided with the representation and acceptance of a benevolent whereas *Poltergeist* presents the 'Other' as a malevolent force looking not to ingrain itself into a family but rather to split it apart.

Canby (1982) again notes that *Poltergeist* uses the representation of the fantastical, the unexplained, and the corruption of childhood wishes and dreams as fears made manifest as a prism to discuss the wider societal and political change being seen in America during the late 1970s and early 1980s. Bradshaw (2016), however, states that *Poltergeist* provides an interesting perspective as the director was not within the Hollywood clique, but rather an outsider whose counter-culture perspectives on modern cultural phenomena such as the rise of globalisation and America's unhealthy appetite for consumerism and gentrification provide the film with a nihilistic tone.

According to Brehmer (2018), *Poltergeist* provides commentary on the tribulations of the early 1980s American middle-class's suburban life, colonialism, and the perceived break-down of the nuclear family unit via the damaging excesses of capitalism and consumerism suggesting that *Poltergeist* (among others) represents social traumas subtly being played out as thinly veiled metaphors for an American middle-class trying to come to grips with a disastrous and stressful time of post-Vietnam society. Kellner (1983a) backs up this discussion, noting the film was released into 'an atmosphere of fear and trembling in the age of Reagan'.

POLTERGEIST

Richard Corliss (1982) through Time magazine, notes that *Poltergeist* is a *'sly comedy'* supporting the 'proposition that violence on TV...or precisely, in it, can have an influence on children who watch it', noting, for example, the breakfast scene where Carol Anne is staring straight at the static at the television and without noticing Diane turns the channel over showing a Western shoot-out instead. This reinforces Hooper's themes of the desensitisation of a consumer audience both to content and violence, which is ironic as he himself propagated texts that are renowned, as the BFI note, for pushing the boundaries of taste and decency.

Finally, a critique presented by Kendrick (2009) from within the ironically titled *Hollywood Bloodshed: Violence in 1980s American Cinema* notes that *Poltergeist* is a text that reinforces the emphasis of the reunification of families—an apt and fitting quote that sums up concisely the 'American Dream' so often represented within 'Spielberigan' texts.

7.3 THE FILM'S CURSE

One of the more compelling issues surrounding the film and its meta-narrative is that the film is supposedly cursed. While the notion of *'cursed celluloid'* has been used to promote films for decades, ranging from the beginnings of horror cinema with *Häxan* (1922) through to more knowing and audience-savvy texts such as *In the Mouth of Madness* (1994), *Ringu/The Ring, Cigarette Burns* (2005) and, more recently, *Antrum: The Deadliest Film Ever Made* (2018), the mystique that a film is something more than just what is on-screen is intriguing and the 'curse' that *Poltergeist* has nurtured within the cultural consciousness arguably has far more resonance than the manufactured attempts of other films' 'meta-narratives' delivered through viral advertising, public relations, or marketing campaigns.

The initial, unintentional, use of 'meta-narrative' (the interpretation of events and circumstances surrounding a media production) of *Poltergeist* developed due to a series of co-incidental factual events occurring in and around the time of the film's initial release. These events heightened greatly the extent to which the press and critics and in turn the public engaged with the film. The 'curse' while not initially advocated by the distributors at the time became an urban legend that was (ethically or not) embraced over time in the drive to push up the box office takings and of course to be highlighted and debated upon though the past decades' ancillary markets of VHS, DVD, Blu-ray, and broadcast as well as an episode of E! Hollywood Story specifically focusing on the film's notoriety.

The evolution of the film's 'curse' resonates from numerous points of origin and while the deaths of some actors associated with the film were folded into and attributed to the film's 'meta-narrative' and subsequent mythology over time (most notably that of Will Sampson, who played Taylor, and Julian Beck, who played Reverend Henry Kane in the film's sequels) the early passing of two of the main actresses of the film at a young age became triggers for the film's notoriety.

The death of Dominique Dunne who played Dana can't be associated with the film's supernatural subject matter in any way. The actress was tragically murdered by her boyfriend John Sweeney, who strangled Dunne into unconsciousness, after which she spent four days in a coma before finally dying on 4 November 1982, almost five months to the day from the film's US release on 4 June.

Heather O'Rourke, who played Carol Anne, also passed away at an early age (12) when she was misdiagnosed with Crohn's disease in 1987. The following year, O'Rourke fell ill again, and her symptoms were casually attributed to the flu. A day later, she collapsed and suffered a cardiac arrest and septic shock during an operation to correct a bowel obstruction from a congenital undiagnosed intestinal abnormality. Her death came four months before the release of *Poltergeist III*.

While the deaths of two of the lead actresses cannot be attributed to the film's production, the 'curse' motif and legacy gained traction when it was reported that Oliver Robbins (Robbie) had been choked by the possessed clown toy during production and was unable to breathe as the mechanisms proved to be too tight and restrictive. The film's infamy also carried over into its sequels, where an exorcism was conducted on the set of the film. Will Sampson, a member of the Muscogee (Creek) Nation, who played shaman Taylor in the movie, was very concerned about the use of skeletons in the first film and as such performed the ceremony on the behest of the crew members.

POLTERGEIST

7.4 THE REAL CORPSES

Sampson's exorcism on the set of the second film was not done without justification or reasoning as the fact that real skeletons were indeed used in the film's final swimming pool sequence. Assistant prop master Bruce Kasson noted during a VH1's I Love the '80s video interview, 'Yes, the skeletons were real…they came from Carolina Biological' a medical and science supply company that sold human skeletons. Kassons continues, 'Replica skeletons did not exist, as far as I remember, at that time.' Companies such as Carolina Biological provided real corpses to be used for use in medical schools with real skeletons being considerably cheaper to get hold of than model versions. Special effects makeup artist Craig Reardon backed up the comment, stating, 'I acquired a number of actual biological surgical skeletons is what they're called. They're for hanging in classrooms in study. These are actual skeletons from people. I think the bones are acquired from India.'

Actress Jo-Beth Williams was unaware of this and while filming the pool scenes did not know that the bodies were real skeletons, explaining in an interview in 2008 for *TV Land: Myths & Legends*:

> In my innocence and naiveté, I assumed that these were not real skeletons. I assumed that they were prop skeletons made out of plastic or rubber. I found out—as did the whole crew—that they were using real skeletons, because it's far too expensive to make fake skeletons out of rubber. And I think everybody got real creeped out by the idea of that.

While she was initially unaware that the bodies in the pool were real, she was more hesitant about the swimming pool scene due to the large amount of live electrical equipment needed in and around the set, positioned over and around the pool. In an anecdote Spielberg is said to have jumped in the pool himself, noting, 'Now if a light falls in, we will both fry.'

7.5 CINEMATOGRAPHY AND STRUCTURAL COLLAPSE

In *Poltergeist*'s attempts to visualise the spirits, scenarios, and nightmarish creatures from the 'Other Side', the film justifies its BAFTA award and its Oscar nomination. Released well before the reliance on computer-generated imagery (CGI), all of the effects in *Poltergeist* were achieved either using physical effects (i.e., on set) or optical effects during post-production.

These elements of the film were overseen by visual effects master Richard Edlund (*Raiders of the Lost Ark*, etc.) and his effects company Boss Films, which went on to produce practical effects for other supernatural-themed films such as *Ghostbusters*, *Fright Night*, and *Big Trouble in Little China* (1986). Applying a similar aesthetic to represent the supernatural on *Poltergeist* as he did on *Raiders of the Lost Ark*, Edlund's team utilised water tanks, oils, paint, and colouring to give the effects of the fluidic unnatural storms presented in purple and black bruising colours looming above the Freeling house to contrast with shots of clear summer evening Californian skies.

Water, over-saturated lighting, and contrast are also to great effect in presenting the unnatural look of the spirts within the film. As with *Raiders*, the use of shooting the ghost models covered in loose material (such as textiles, fabric, and even toilet paper) gives a perfect representation of the unearthly, an ethereal translucent look that has the edges of the spirts dissipating and dissolving as they floated and separated in the water.

Figure 7.1. Final scene

Adding additional matted coloured optical effects to represent spectral orbs to these scenes combined with the intense backlights and over-saturated brilliant white/strobe effects Spielberg utilised on-set and in-camera enhances the unnatural, unearthly apparitions of the spirits. Placing them in scenes set full of a natural light and a colour

POLTERGEIST

palette of oranges and yellows to represent the warmth of a familiar suburban household makes the effects produced more unnerving.

This familiar setting of the Freeling house itself is also part of the visual effect landscape of the film and does not itself come away unscathed. The interior of the house was a set built on a soundstage with the rooms of the house being constructed next to one another with the intent to utilise the environment to assist the visual effects crew in the presentation of the manifestations of the spirits. Holes were cut in kitchen floors (to pull Carol Anne across) and cabinets and kitchen tops were adapted to allow rod-puppeteers in to move steaks across surfaces or for models to be made to allow for crew and actors (or, in the case of Marty gouging at his own face, Spielberg himself) to interact with stunt-people, models, and other cumbersome practical effects. The most elaborate of these was the parental bedroom, which was built on hydraulics to allow it to be rotated (similar to the one used on *2001: A Space Odyssey*), to give the scene where Diane is molested by the poltergeists and forced up the wall and onto the ceiling an uncanny effect without the requirement of visible harnesses and cabling.

For one of the most memorable and showcased visual effects shots of the film, in which the Freeling home implodes, a six-foot model scale of the Freeling home was constructed. The effects team used concealed triggered wires and pulleys threaded throughout the house, which were then placed on a high-powered vacuum machine with the camera locked in place above it all. When the signal was given, wires were pulled to trigger the collapse and the vacuum turned, giving the effect of the house folding in on itself and the subsequent debris sucked away into nothingness. The scale model took four months to create and a further two months of additional optical and post-production work to perfect the effect costing more than $25,000 to create. Filmed at 300 frames-per-second, the effect was slowed down by 15 times for the final version, capped by the addition of a small white/blue light, intended to present the turning off of a television set. After the intricate model was destroyed, its fragments were gathered up and placed in a Perspex box that (supposedly) Spielberg has on display in his office.

To add to the effective use of visual effects to portray a landscape of the unnatural and uncanny Jerry Goldsmith's music and score for *Poltergeist* can also be credited for creating an equally unique and unnerving audio experience for the film. Goldsmith had

107

scored genre films such as *Logan's Run* (1977), *Star Trek: The Motion Picture* (1979), and *The Omen Trilogy* (1976–1981), and with *Poltergeist* crafted a slow almost meandering title theme (entitled 'Carol Anne's Theme'), reminiscent of a child's simplistic piano recital. The film score is not built on shocks or archetypal traditional horror clichés of tinkering pianos or distorted bowing strings of a double bass but rather is constructed to be child-like and innocent, which itself has become something of an audio horror cliché (children's laughter, nursey rhymes, and vocal distortion overlaid into scores). That is not to say the score does not induce scares and it is not without audio triggers: at the initial appearance of the poltergeist reaching for Carol Anne from the television the audio 'jump-scare' is hugely effective.

The other iconic and recognisable audio effect from the film is the much repeated (and indeed parodied) audio distortion done to represent Carol Anne's entrapment on the 'Other Side'—her voice is electronically pulled and stretched, processed through an electronic filter that adds an unnerving, manufactured, and intentionally artificial tone. She is trapped in a non-place, a void filled with the static and the spiritual, a lost little girl panicking in an unknown, unnatural, and wholly alien place.

7.6 CULTURAL RESONANCE

For all its triple Academy Award nominations (Sound, Visual Effects and Original Score), Saturn and BAFTA wins, *Poltergeist* was undeniably overshadowed by the phenomenal worldwide success of its counterpart film *E.T. Poltergeist* was a commercial and critical success, yet the timing of the film's release, in the middle of summer and only a week before the release of *E.T.* (11 June, 1982) arguably suppressed takings for the film through the rest of the summer with Spielberg's other, more uplifting suburban narrative taking more than $350 million dollars in North America in its first theatrical run, leaving *Poltergeist* to become the eighth highest grossing film of 1982 in the US, with a still impressive $76,606,280 (Box-office Mojo).

However, the success of *Poltergeist* cannot only be measured by its initial impact of box-office takings. Arguably, over time the film has proved to be more culturally significant than its extra-terrestrial counterpart in providing more impactful and permanent marks on the 'pop culture' psyche than the benevolent alien botanist.

POLTERGEIST

The film's iconic image of Carol Anne silhouetted in front of the static-filled television screen (designed by cinema poster artist Carl Ramsey) has become one of the most recognisable film posters of all time and has produced a multitude of homages, pastiche, and parodies appearing in texts such as *Scary Movie 2* (2001) and *ParaNorman* (2012). Television shows such as *South Park*, *Family Guy*, *American Dad*, and *The Simpsons* have also parodied the film, as well as it being a focal point for a stand-up routine for comedian Eddie Murphy.

Figure 7.2. The Simpsons' *parody*

The film is also significant in the continued propagation of the notion of a 'Haunted Indian Burial Ground' motif. However, the Freeling house is *not* actually built on sacred native American land at all. Plot-wise this is factually misconstrued due to a minor plot detail—the Freeling house was built on a graveyard and the connection to Indian burial grounds comes in part through Teague's speech to Steve in a scene where they are both looking down on the estate from the hills overlooking the estate and he notes, 'Besides, it's not ancient tribal burial ground, it's just people.' This misconception and misinterpretation while minor did not stop Seth McFarlane from having either Peter Griffin use a dug-up native American skull as a protective cup or Stewie Griffin use his abduction in the same episode of *Family Guy* entitled 'Petergeist' to sing Phil Collins'

109

songs in homage to the reverberated voice the sound designers of *Poltergeist* used to portray Carol Anne's communication from the 'Other Side'.

The cultural significance of *Poltergeist* has also not just been felt within America, as broadcasts such as the BBC produced *Ghostwatch* (1992) share similarities to the plot of the film. As *Ghostwatch* writer Stephen Volk notes, 'Ghosts no longer inhabit stately homes or rattle chains. They live in ordinary council houses.'

The text has also permitted genre directors to produce darker material that, rather than concentrating on the subversive or humour found in the film, have instead concentrated on the notions of loss, trauma and violation, with films such as *Insidious* (2010) and *Paranormal Activity* (2009). These utilise the domestic setting, underlying themes, and context of *Poltergeist* to explore these aspects further, reinforcing *Poltergeist*'s claim to be somewhat of a template of the 'suburban haunted house genre'.

7.7 CONCLUSIONS

Poltergeist still scares—and as such still holds significant cultural resonance and retains an influence on modern filmmaking. It is a film that contextually is a paradox, invoking both aspects of fear and celebration and provides a rich viewing experience full of jump scares and wonderment. With the surrounding mythology and meta-text of the film *Poltergeist* has earned its place as a significant part of the tapestry of modern horror lore. It is a film that, like *Jaws* and *Jurassic Park* (1993), provided legitimate foundation points for genre movies and, like these cultural cornerstones, was, hardly coincidentally, overseen by the creative hand of Steven Spielberg.

Poltergeist can also be regarded as a 'gateway text' to horror—a film that has introduced filmmakers, critics, and scholars alike into the wide and appealing realms of horror cinema. A well-designed, intelligent, and visually stunning film it has proven to be a perennial text that has generated sequels, remakes, and a television series, all of which have added to the lore of the franchise. However, no matter the number of remakes or reimaginings nothing stands up to the Illicit fear induced by being told, 'They're here.'

BIBLIOGRAPHY

Arnett, R. (2006) 'Eighties Noir: The Dissenting Voice in Reagan's America', *Journal of Popular Film and Television*, Volume 3, Issue 34, pp. 123–129.

Arnold, S. (2013) *Maternal Horror Film: Melodrama and Motherhood* (Palgrave Macmillan).

Badley, L. (1995) *Film, Horror and the Body Fantastic* (Greenwood Publishing Group).

Bala, M. (2010) 'The Clown: An Archetypal Self-journey', *Jung Journal*, Volume 4, Issue 1, pp. 50–71.

Barthes, R. (2009) *Mythologies* (Random House Vintage Classics).

Bassett, N. (2020) *Dead Zones: A Phenomenology of Disconnection* (University of Illinois at Chicago Publishing).

Beard, D. (2015) 'Horror Movies at Home: Supernatural Horror, Delivery Systems and 1980s Satanic Panic', *Horror Studies*, Volume 6, Issue 2, pp. 211–223.

Beauregard, R. (2006) *When America Became Suburban* (University of Minnesota Press).

Becker, M. (2006) 'A Point of Little Hope: Hippie Horror Films and the Politics of Ambivalence', *The Velvet Light Trap*, Volume 1, Issue 57, pp. 42–59.

Beebe, J. (1983) 'Review of Poltergeist', *The San Francisco Jung Institute Library Journal*, Volume 4, Issue 2, pp. 54–62.

Benchoff, H. (2014) *A Companion to the Horror Film* (John Wiley and Sons).

Beville, M. (2013) *The Unnameable Monster in Literature and Film* (Routledge).

Blanco, M.D. & Peeren, E. (2013) *The spectralities reader: ghosts and haunting in contemporary cultural theory* (Bloomsbury).

Bloom, J. (2004) 'They Came. They Sawed', *Texas Monthly*, Issue 32. https://www.texasmonthly.com/arts-entertainment/they-came-they-sawed/.

Bradshaw, P. (2016) 'From Notting Hill to Poltergeist: How Hollywood Handles Gentrification', *The Guardian*. https://www.theguardian.com/cities/2016/oct/03/from-notting-hill-to-poltergeist-how-the-movies-handle-gentrification.

DEVIL'S ADVOCATES

Brehmer, N. (2018) *How Poltergeist Destroyed the American Dream (And Why That's Great)*. https://wickedhorror.com/features/retrospectives/how-poltergeist-destroys-the-american-dream-and-why-thats-great/.

Brook, C. (2001) 'The Personal Touch—Jack Valenti has fought Hollywood's battles in Washington for thirty-five years. Can he still get his way?' *New Yorker*. https://www.newyorker.com/magazine/2001/08/13/the-personal-touch-3.

Buckland, W. (2006) *Directed by Steven Spielberg: Poetics of the Contemporary Hollywood Blockbuster* (Continuum International Publishing Group).

Burgess, J. (1987) 'Landscapes in the Living-room: Television and Landscape Research', *Landscape Research*, Volume 12, Issue 3, pp. 1–7.

Canby, V. (1982) 'Poltergeist, from Spielberg—It's a Film in which Childhood Wishes and Fears are Made Manifest', *The New York Times*. https://www.nytimes.com/1982/06/04/movies/poltergeist-from-spielberg.html.

Castelli, S. (2017) 'It's All Fun and Games until the Laughter Ceases', *Variations*, Volume 25, Issue 1, pp. 73–85.

Chaston, J. (1997) 'The "Ozification" of American Children's Fantasy Films: The Blue Bird, Alice in Wonderland, and Jumanji', *Children's Literature Association Quarterly Johns Hopkins University Press*, Volume 22, Issue 1, pp. 13–20.

Clover, C.J. (1987) 'Her Body, Himself: Gender in the Slasher Film', *Representations*, Issue 20, Special Issue: Misogyny, Misandry, and Misanthropy, pp. 187–228.

Clover, C.J. (1992) *Men, Women, and Chain Saws: Gender in the Modern Horror Film* (Princeton University Press).

Cohen, L. (2003) *A Consumers' Republic: The Politics of Mass Consumption in Postwar America* (Vintage Books; Illustrated edition).

Corliss, R. (1982) 'Steve's Magic Summer', *Time*. https://time.com/3833695/e-t-poltergeist-Steven-spielberg-movie-review/.

Creed, B. (1993) *The Monstrous Feminine: Film, Feminism, Psychoanalysis* (Routledge).

Creed, B. (1994) *Baby Bitches from Hell: Monstrous Little Women in Film* (Scary Women

Symposium, UCLA: January).

Culver, S. (1988) 'What Manikins Want: The Wonderful Wizard of Oz and The Art of Decorating Dry Goods Windows', *Representations*, Issue 21, pp. 9–16.

Curtis, B. (2008) *Dark Places: The Haunted House in Film* (Reaktion Books).

De Laurentis, T. (1985) *Alice Doesn't: Feminism, Semiotics, Cinema* (Indiana University Press).

Del Pilar Blanko, M. & Peen, E. (2013) *The Spectralities Reader: Ghosts and Haunting in Contemporary Cultural Theory* (Bloomsbury Academic).

Derry, C. (2009) *Dark Dreams 2.0: A Psychological History of the Modern Horror Film from the 1950s to the 21st Century* (McFarlane & Co.).

Donato. T. (2000) *The Final Girl: A Few Thoughts on Feminism and Horror*. https://offscreen.com/view/feminism_and_horror.

Doyle, M. (2012) 'The Spirits of '82', *Rue Morgue Magazine*, Issue 121, pp. 16–22.

Durwin, J. (2004) 'Coulrophobia and the Trickster', *Trickster's Way*, Volume 31, Issue 2, Article 4. https://digitalcommons.trinity.edu/trickstersway/vol3/iss1/4.

Dyer, R. (1986) *Heavenly Bodies: Film Stars and Society* (Macmillian).

Ebert, R. (1996) *Night of the Hunter*. https://www.rogerebert.com/reviews/great-movie-the-night-of-the-hunter-1955.

Elms, A. (1983) 'Oz in Science Fiction Film', *The Baum Bugle*, Volume 3, Issue 27, pp. 2–7.

Faraci, D. (2012) *Schlock Corridor: Poltergeist 1982 pt 1*. https://birthmoviesdeath.com/2012/01/08/schlock-corridor-poltergeist-1982-part-i.

Fuery, P. (2003) *Madness and the Cinema—Psychoanalysis, Spectatorship and Culture* (Palgrave Macmillan).

Gaiman, N. (2001) *American Gods* (William Morrow).

Gentile, K. (2000) 'Anxious Supernaturalism: An Analytic of the Uncanny', *Gothic Studies*, Volume 2, Issue 1, pp. 23–38.

DEVIL'S ADVOCATES

George, J. & La Manna, R. (2016) *Postmodern Suburban Spaces: Philosophy, Ethics, and Community in Post-War American Fiction* (Palgrave Macmillan).

Gewirtz, J. (1956) 'A Factor Analysis of Some Attention-Seeking Behaviours of Young Children', *Child Development*, Volume 27, Issue 1, pp. 17–36.

Gordon, A. (2008) *Empire of Dreams: The Science Fiction and Fantasy Films of Steven Spielberg* (Rowman and Littlefield).

Graber, D. (1987) 'Television, News without Pictures', *Critical Studies in Mass Communication*, Volume 4, Issue 1, pp. 74–78.

Grant, B. (1996) 'Rich and Strange: The Yuppie Horror Film', *Journal of Film and Video*, Volume 48, Issue 1, pp. 6–19.

Guillory, B. (2002) *Stained Lens: Style as Cultural Signifier in Seventies Horror Films* (Loyola University (New Orleans, Louisiana) Undergraduate dissertation). https://louisianadigitallibrary.org/islandora/object/loyno-etd%3A161.

Hall, J. (2000) 'The Benefits of Hindsight: Re-visions of HUAC and the Film and Television Industries in *The Front* and *Guilty by Suspicion*', *Film Quarterly*, Volume 54, Issue 2, pp. 15–26.

Harper, O. (2013) *Poltergeist Retrospective/Review*. https://www.youtube.com/watch?v=FZY2e2aHpNI.

Hart, A. (2019) 'Transitional Gothic: Hammer's Gothic Revival and New Horror', *Studies in the Fantastic University of Tampa Press*, Issue 6, pp. 1–21.

Heathcote, E. (2014) 'House of Horror: The Role of Domestic Settings in Scary Movies', *Financial Times*, https://www.ft.com/content/7be7df4e-5547-11e4-89e8-00144feab7de.

Hock, D. (1999) *Birth of the Chaordic Age* (Berrett-Koehler).

Hofmann, S. (2008) 'Cognitive Processes during Fear Acquisition and Extinction in Animals and Humans—Implications for Exposure Therapy of Anxiety Disorders', *Clinical Psychology Review*, Volume 28, Issue 2, pp. 199–210.

Iaccino, J. (1994) *Psychological Reflections in Cinematic Terror: Jungian Archetypes in Horror Films* (Praeger).

Jackson, C. (2000) 'Little, Violent, White: The "Bad Seed" and the Matter of Children', *The Journal of Popular Film and Television*, Volume 28, Issue 1, pp. 64–73.

James, D. & Berg, R. (1996) *The Hidden Foundation: Cinema and the Question of Class* (University of Minnesota).

Kahn, J. (1982) *Poltergeist: The Novelisation of the Film* (Harper Collins).

Kallitsis, P. (2018) *The Discourse of Urban Regeneration and Gentrification as Devices of Fear in the Horror Genre* (Portsmouth School of Architecture. Paper presented at International Visual Association 36th Conference).

Kellner, D. (1983a) 'Fear and Trembling in the Age of Reagan: Notes on Poltergeist', *Socialist Review*, Issue 69, pp. 121–131.

Kellner. D. (1983b) 'Poltergeist: Suburban Ideology', *Jump Cut: A Review of Contemporary Media*, Volume 28, Issue 1, pp. 5–6.

Kellner, D. (1983c) 'Critical Theory, Commodities and the Consumer Society', *Theory, Culture & Society*, Volume 1, Issue 3, pp. 66–83.

Kendrick, F. (2009) *Hollywood Bloodshed: Violence in 1980s American Cinema* (Southern Illinois University Press).

Kristeva, J. (1980) *Powers of Horror: An Essay on Abjection* (Le Seuil/Columbia University Press). https://www.csus.edu/indiv/o/obriene/art206/readings/kristeva%20-%20 powers%20of%20horror%5b1%5d.pdf.

Latham, R. (1994) 'Subterranean Suburbia: Underneath the Smalltown Myth in the Two Versions of Invaders from Mars', *ScienceFiction Studies*, Volume 22, Issue 2, pp. 198–208.

Lawrence, J. & Jewett, R. (1977) 'The American Monomyth', *Cross-Currents*, Volume 27, Issue 3, pp. 348–351.

Lee, E. (2016) "'*Poltergeist Scarred Me for Life*'': James Wan on *Saw*'s Torture-porn Label and *The Conjuring 2*'. https://www.scmp.com/culture/film-tv/article/1968040/poltergeist-scarred-me-life-james-wan-saws-torture-porn-label-and.

Leeder, M. (2008) 'The Fall of the House of Meaning: Between Static and Slime in Poltergeist', *The Irish Journal of Gothic and Horror Studies*, Issue 5, n.p. https://

DEVIL'S ADVOCATES

irishgothichorror.files.wordpress.com/2018/03/murrayc2a0leeder.pdf.

Mackley, J.S. (2016) *The Fears of a Clown* (Paper presented at The Dark Fantastic: Sixth Annual Joint Fantasy Symposium, The University of Northampton).

Mandall, P. (1982) '*Poltergeist*: Stilling the Restless Animus', *Cinefex Magazine*, Issue 10, pp. 4–40.

Mander, J. (1978) *Four Arguments for the Elimination of Television* (William Morrow Paperbacks).

Martin, B. (1982) 'Tobe Hooper on *Texas Chainsaw Massacre* and *Poltergeist*', *Fangoria*, Issue 23, pp. 24-28.

McAndrew, F. (2016) *The Psychology Behind Why Clowns Creep Us Out*. https://theconversation.com/the-psychology-behind-why-clowns-creep-us-out-65936.

McBride, J. (1987) *Steven Spielberg: A Biography* (Faber and Faber).

McFadzean, A. (2017) 'The Suburban Fantastic: A Semantic and Syntactic Grouping in Contemporary Hollywood Cinema', *Science Fiction Film & Television*, Volume 10, Issue 1, pp. 1–25.

McFadzean, A. (2019) *Suburban Fantastic Cinema: Growing Up in the Late Twentieth Century* (Wallflower/Columbia University Press).

Medved, H. (2010) *Location Filming in Los Angeles* (Arcadia Publishing).

Mehls, R. (2015) *In History No One Can Hear You Scream: Feminism and the Horror Film 1974–1996* (Art History Theses & Dissertations, Master's dissertation). https://scholar.colorado.edu/concern/graduate_thesis_or_dissertations/jw827c00x.

Merish, L. (1996) 'Cuteness and Commodity Aesthetics: Tom Thumb and Shirley Temple', in R. Garland (ed.), *Freakery: Cultural Spectacles of the Extraordinary Body* (New York University Press), pp. 185–205.

Michelson S. (2018) *Terror in the Cul-de-sac: The Suburban Uncanny in Late 20th Century American Horror* (Honors Thesis Collection—Wellesley College, undergraduate dissertation).

Miller, J. (2007) "'Now That I Have It, I Don't Want It''. Vocation and Obligation in Contemporary Hollywood Ghost Films', in Sharon R. Sherman and Mikel J. Koven (eds), *Folklore/Cinema: Popular Vernacular Cinema* (Utah State University Press), pp. 113–128.

Miller, C. (2013) *Undead in the West II: They Just Keep Coming* (Scarecrow Press).

Morton, J. (2016) *1980s Cinema and the Disturbing Side of Suburbia.* https://lwlies.com/articles/1980s-american-suburbia-in-film/.

Muir, J.K. (2002) *Eaten Alive at a Chainsaw Massacre: The Films of Tobe Hooper* (McFarland & Co.).

Muir, J.K. (2007) *Horror Films of the 1980s* (McFarland & Co.).

Mulvey, L. (1975) 'Visual Pleasure and Narrative Cinema', *Screen*, Volume 16, Issue 3, pp. 6–18.

Mulvey, L. (1996) *Fetishism and Curiosity* (BFI Publishing; First Edition).

Mulvey-Roberts, M. (1998) *The Handbook of the Gothic* (Palgrave Macmillan).

Murphy, B. (2009) *The Suburban Gothic in American Popular Culture* (Palgrave Macmillan).

Muzzio, D. & Halper, T. (2002) 'PLEASANTVILLE? The Suburb and its Representation in American Movies', *Urban Affairs Review*, Volume 37, Issue 4, pp. 543–574.

Myers, W. (1976) 'Imaginary Companions, Fantasy Twins, Mirror Dreams and Depersonalisation', *The Psychoanalytic Quarterly*, Volume 45, Issue 4, pp. 503–524.

Nakagawa, C. (2017) 'Dangers Inside the Home: Rereading Haunted House Films from a Gothic Perspective', *Journal of American and Canadian Studies*, Issue 35, pp. 75–96.

Neale, S. (1999) *Genre and Hollywood* (Routledge).

Newman, K. (1988) *Nightmare Movies: A Critical History of the Horror Film, 1968–88* (Bloomsbury).

Pollock, D. (1982) '*Poltergeist*: Just Whose Film is It?', *Los Angeles Times*, Monday, 24 May, https://www.newspapers.com/clip/94850743/the-los-angeles-times/.

Poltergeist Pressbook (1982) https://www.zomboscloset.com/zombos_closet_of_horror_b/2017/07/poltergeist-1982-pressbook.html.

Radford, B. (2016) *Bad Clowns* (University of New Mexico Press).

Rowley, S. (2015) *Movie Towns and Sitcom Suburbs: Building Hollywood's Ideal Communities* (Palgrave Macmillan).

Soares, A. (2014) 'Top 100 Horror Movies of All Time: From *Psycho* to *Edith Scob*', *Alt Film Guide*. https://www.altfg.com/film/top-100-horror-movies/.

Schneider, S. (1999) 'Monsters as (Uncanny) Metaphors: Freud, Lakoff, and the Representation of Monstrosity in Cinematic Horror', *Other Voices*, Volume 1, Issue 3, n.p. http://www.othervoices.org/1.3/sschneider/monsters.php.

Schober, A. (2016) *Children in the Films of Steven Spielberg* (Lexington Books).

Sconce, J. (2000) *Haunted Media: Electronic Presence from Telegraphy to Television* (Duke University Press).

Scott, N. (2007) *Monsters and the Monstrous: Myths and Metaphors of Enduring Evil* (Rodopi).

Sellars, J. (2014) *Light Shining in a Dark Place: Discovering Theology through Film* (Pickwick Publications).

Sharrett, C. (2009) 'The Problem of Saw: "Torture Porn" and the Conservatism of Contemporary Horror Films', *Cineaste Winter*, Volume 35, Issue 1, pp. 32–37.

Shengold, M. (1974) 'The Metaphor of the Mirror', *Journal of the American Psychoanalytic Association*, Volume 22, Issue 1, pp. 97–115.

Sherman, S.R. & Koven, M.J. (2007) *Folklore/Cinema: Popular Film as Vernacular Culture* (Utah State University Press).

Spence, L. (2006) *Encyclopaedia of Occultism* (Cosimo Classics).

Spiegel, L. (1992) *Make Room for TV: Television and the Family Ideal in Postwar America* (University of Chicago Press).

Spigel, L. & McChesny, R. (1993) *Seducing the Innocent: Television and Childhood in 1950s Television: New Perspectives in U.S. Communication History* (University of Minnesota Press).

Stott, A. (2012) 'Clowns on the Verge of a Nervous Breakdown: Dickens, Coulrophobia, and the Memoirs of Joseph Grimaldi', *Journal for Early Modern Cultural Studies*, Volume 12, Issue 4, pp. 3–25.

Subissati, A. (2010) *When There's No More Room in Hell: The Sociology of the Living Dead* (LAP LAMBERT Academic Publishing).

Tobias, S. (2007) 'Poltergeist: 25th Anniversary Edition', *AV Club*. https://www.avclub.com/poltergeist-25th-anniversary-edition-1798203255.

Troxclair, M. (2013) 'The Legend of the Pied Piper in the Nineteenth and Twentieth Centuries: Grimm, Browning, and Skurzynski', *Looking Glass: New Perspectives on Children's Literature*, Volume 17, Issue 1. http://www.lib.latrobe.edu.au/ojs/index.php/tlg/article/view/390/383.

Tudor, A. (1989) *Monsters and Mad Scientists: A Cultural History of the Horror Movie* (John Wiley & Sons).

Tudor, A. (1997) 'Why Horror? The Peculiar Pleasures of a Popular Genre', *Cultural Studies*, Volume 11, Issue 3, pp. 443–463.

Wallace, D. (2004) 'Uncanny Stories: The Ghost Story as Female Gothic', *Gothic Studies*, Volume 23, Issue 1, pp. 57–68.

Waller, G. (1987) *American Horrors: Essays on the Modern American Horror Film* (University of Illinois Press)

Weinstock, J. & Lauro, S. (2017) *Zombie Theory: A Reader* (University of Minnesota).

Williams, T. (2014) *Hearths of Darkness: The Family in the American Horror Film* (University Press of Mississippi).

Wood, R. (1986) *Hollywood—From Vietnam to Reagan* (Columbia University Press).

Zakarin, J. (2015) 'Inside the Hell House of the Original 'Poltergeist'. https://www.yahoo.com/entertainment/making-of-poltergeist-original-film-120040571057.html.

Zinoman, J. (2013) *Shock Value* (Gerald Duckworth & Co Ltd.).

Printed and bound by CPI Group (UK) Ltd, Croydon, CR0 4YY

09/07/2023

03233882-0001